# Marzano Research Development Team

**Director of Publications**

Julia A. Simms

**Production Editor**

Laurel Hecker

**Editorial Assistants/Staff Writers**

Ming Lee Newcomb

Elizabeth A. Bearden

**Marzano Research Associates**

Tina Boogren

Bev Clemens

Jane Doty Fischer

Jeff Flygare

Tammy Heflebower

Mitzi Hoback

Jan K. Hoegh

Russell Jenson

Jessica Kanold-McIntyre

Sonny Magaña

Margaret McInteer

Diane E. Paynter

Kristin Poage

Salle Quackenboss

Cameron Rains

Tom Roy

Gerry Varty

Phil Warrick

Kenneth C. Williams

Visit **marzanoresearch.com/reproducibles** to download the reproducibles in this book.

# Table of Contents

# Chapter 3

# Chapter 4

# About the Authors

**Robert J. Marzano, PhD,** is the co-founder and CEO of Marzano Research in Denver, Colorado. During his forty-seven years in the field of education, he has worked with educators as a speaker and trainer and has authored more than forty books and 250 articles on topics such as instruction, assessment, writing and implementing standards, cognition, effective leadership, and school intervention. His books include *The Art and Science of Teaching, Leaders of Learning, On Excellence in Teaching, Effective Supervision, The Classroom Strategies Series, Using Common Core Standards to Enhance Classroom Instruction and Assessment, Vocabulary for the Common Core, Vocabulary for the New Science Standards, Teacher Evaluation That Makes a Difference, A Handbook for High Reliability Schools*, and *Awaken the Learner*. His practical translations of the most current research and theory into classroom strategies are known internationally and are widely practiced by both teachers and administrators. He received a bachelor's degree from Iona College in New York, a master's degree from Seattle University, and a doctorate from the University of Washington.

**Jana S. Marzano, MA,** is a psychotherapist in private practice in Denver, Colorado. For the past thirty years, she has specialized in helping those suffering from post-traumatic stress disorder, mood disorders, marital issues, and substance and behavioral addictions. She works extensively with children and adolescents and is the coauthor of numerous articles and several books on topics ranging from classroom management to the role of the self-system in determining human behavior. She received her bachelor's degree in human services from Metropolitan State College in Denver and her master's degree in agency counseling from the University of Northern Colorado.

# *About Marzano Research*

Marzano Research is a joint venture between Solution Tree and Dr. Robert J. Marzano. Marzano Research combines Dr. Marzano's forty years of educational research with continuous action research in all major areas of schooling in order to provide effective and accessible instructional strategies, leadership strategies, and class-room assessment strategies that are always at the forefront of best practice. By providing such an all-inclusive research-into-practice resource center, Marzano Research provides teachers and principals the tools they need to effect profound and immediate improvement in student achievement.

**Leabharlann James Hardiman**

Chun seiceáil cathain atá an leabhar seo le tabhairt ar ais agat, nó chun an leabhar a athnuachan, féach ar do chuntas leabharlainne.

To check when this book is due back or to renew it please check your Library Account.

**http://tinyurl.com/NUIGLibraryAccount**

Gearrann an leabharlann fíneálacha as leabhair a thugtar ar ais go mall.

A fine will be charged for books returned after their due date.

# *Preface*

To a great degree, we have been writing this book for about three decades. In the mid-1980s we came to the joint realization that the field of education (Bob's focus) and the field of clinical psychology (Jana's focus) would both be enhanced by a comprehensive theory of how the human mind operates. It was at that time that we began crafting the model presented in this book—a model driven by research and theory that explains how human beings operate on a moment-by-moment basis.

The heart of that model is the interaction among three dynamic processes: (1) our emotional responses, (2) our interpretations, and (3) our actions. Of these processes, our interpretations are the fulcrum. They are the source of our emotional reactions and our actions. The interplay of these three processes constitutes the "inner world" of human experience. It is a world in which we spend the majority of our time. It defines what we believe, how we behave, and who we are in relation to the people, events, and tasks we encounter in the outside world.

Understanding the inner world gives us control over it. This book is written specifically to and for classroom teachers with the intent of providing them with a means of understanding how and why they react to specific situations in specific ways. This knowledge provides them with the awareness and skills to ensure that all students are not only treated fairly and kindly, but in a manner that motivates and inspires them. While the information presented in this book has an obvious connection to effective classroom management, it also has implications for a much broader view of curriculum, instruction, and assessment. Finally, it has implications for how our lives might be approached outside of the classroom.

—Robert J. Marzano and
Jana S. Marzano

# Chapter 1

## *Understanding the Inner World*

It is a widely accepted fact that what teachers do in their classrooms can have a substantial effect on the learning of their students. If teachers engage in specific behaviors and employ specific strategies, their students tend to learn better than if they do not use those strategies. Consider the strategy of activating prior knowledge: if teachers help students recall and discuss what they already know about a topic before presenting new information regarding that topic, students tend to learn that information more readily. This applies to other strategies as well: if teachers help students generate graphic representations for what they are studying, they tend to learn the content better; if teachers expose students to content multiple times, they tend to learn it better; and so on.

There is a vast research and theory base around the teacher behaviors and instructional strategies that show promise in enhancing students' learning. Reviews of such behaviors and strategies have been chronicled in a number of books, such as the following:

- *High-Impact Instruction: A Framework for Great Teaching* (Knight, 2013)

- *Visible Learning for Teachers: Maximizing Impact on Learning* (Hattie, 2012)

- *Instruction That Measures Up: Successful Teaching in the Age of Accountability* (Popham, 2009)

- *The Skillful Teacher: Building Your Teaching Skills, 6th ed.* (Saphier, Haley-Speca, & Gower, 2008)
- *Enhancing Professional Practice: A Framework for Teaching, 2nd ed.* (Danielson, 2007)
- *The Art and Science of Teaching: A Comprehensive Framework for Effective Instruction* (Marzano, 2007)
- *The Strategic Teacher: Selecting the Right Research-Based Strategy for Every Lesson* (Silver, Strong, & Perini, 2007)
- *Teaching With the Brain in Mind, 2nd and rev. ed.* (Jensen, 2005)
- *Understanding by Design, 2nd ed.* (Wiggins & McTighe, 2005)
- *What Works in Schools: Translating Research into Action* (Marzano, 2003b)
- *Classroom Instruction That Works: Research-Based Strategies for Increasing Student Achievement* (Marzano, Pickering, & Pollock, 2001)

While it will always be important to keep abreast of teaching behaviors and instructional strategies that have the greatest chance of enhancing students' learning, there is another aspect of effective teaching that has been virtually ignored in the literature on classroom instruction: the relationship between what teachers are thinking and feeling at any point in time and their actions at that same point in time. Historically this issue has been largely ignored, although recent years have seen calls for including the management of thoughts and emotions in the discussion of effective teaching. As Daniel Liston and Jim Garrison (2004) noted:

> For too long we have left emotions in the ontological basement of educational scholarship, to be dragged up and out only when a particular topic necessitated it (e.g., classroom management, student motivation, or teacher 'burnout'). That seems ill advised, and it is time to rebuild our academic house. When we teach, we teach with ideas and feelings. When we interact with students, we react and they respond with thoughts and emotions. (pp. 4–5)

Evidence within education is beginning to mount that the thoughts and emotions of both students and teachers play a critical role in the teaching and learning process. Reviews of research and theory as to the importance of thoughts and emotions in teaching are found in works by Izhak Berkovich and Ori Eyal (2014); Paul W. Richardson, Stuart A. Karabenick, and Helen M. G. Watt (2014); and Paul A. Schutz and Reinhard Pekrun (2007).

Andy Hargreaves (1998) framed the importance of thought and emotion quite eloquently. He stated:

- Teaching is an *emotional practice*.

- Teaching and learning involve *emotional understanding*.

- Teaching is a form of *emotional labour*.

- Teachers' emotions are inseparable from their *moral purposes* and their ability to achieve those purposes.

- Teachers' emotions are rooted in and affect their *selves,* identities and relationships with others.

- Teachers' emotions are shaped by experiences of *power* and powerlessness.

- Teachers' emotions vary with *culture and context*. (p. 319)

The importance of thought and emotion is also quite evident in the general literature on human behavior. To illustrate, in 2003, F. Dan Richard, Charles F. Bond Jr., and Juli J. Stokes-Zoota conducted a meta-analysis of research in psychology spanning one hundred years. Their findings were reported in the article "One Hundred Years of Social Psychology Quantitatively Described." A selection of their many findings is reported in table 1.1 (page 4).

The findings in table 1.1 are organized into two broad categories. The first section reports the findings of studies demonstrating consistency between people's attitudes and their behavior. That section lists five reports, each of which is a synthesis of multiple studies. For example, the first report (Kim & Hunter, 1993a) summarized 138 studies. The *r* stands for a correlation coefficient, which is a

**Table 1.1: Selected Findings From Richard, Bond, and Stokes-Zoota (2003) Meta-Analysis**

| Relationship | n | r | SD |
|---|---|---|---|
| There is consistency between people's attitudes and behavior. | | | |
| Kim & Hunter, 1993a | 138 | .47 | .14 |
| Kim & Hunter, 1993b | 92 | .65 | .14 |
| Kraus, 1995 | 88 | .38 | .18 |
| Farley, Lehmann, & Ryan, 1981 | 37 | .45 | .46 |
| Zimmerman & Vernberg, 1994 | 15 | .43 | — |
| There is consistency between what people intend to do and what they do. | | | |
| Randall & Wolff, 1994 | 98 | .45 | .19 |
| Sheppard, Hartwick, & Warshaw, 1988 | 87 | .53 | .20 |
| Kim & Hunter, 1993b | 47 | .46 | .21 |
| Zimmerman & Vernberg, 1994 | 13 | .56 | — |

Note: n *means number of studies,* r *means correlation, and* SD *means standard deviation.*

measure of the relationship between two variables—in this case, people's attitudes toward a given situation and how they behave in that situation. The correlations reported in that section of table 1.1 range from .38 to .65. Typically, such a range is considered to indicate a medium to strong relationship between the two variables (Cohen, 1988). Taking these findings at face value, it would be safe to conclude that our attitudes are related to our behaviors—if we have positive attitudes about football games, we will likely act in a positive way when attending a football game.

The second section reports the findings of studies demonstrating the consistency between what people intend to do and what they actually do. Again, the correlations are medium to large; it would be safe to conclude that if we intend to work hard on a particular day, we will likely put energy into our work on that day.

In effect, there is a viable research and theory base in the literature on education and psychology supporting the fact that what teachers think and how they feel have an impact on what they do. Stated differently, the "inner world" of teachers' thoughts and feelings affects the "outer world" of their behaviors, which in turn influences students' learning. In this book, we take the position that if teachers understand and monitor their inner worlds, it might go a long way toward enhancing the effectiveness of their outer worlds—their classroom behaviors and use of instructional strategies. This is a topic that, at best, has not been fully explored and, at worst, has been ignored. We begin by exploring the inner world of teaching.

## The Inner World of Teaching

The dynamics of the inner world of teaching are depicted in figure 1.1 (page 6). This model has emerged over a number of decades in our joint research and writings (Marzano, 2003a; Marzano, Gaddy, Foseid, Foseid, & Marzano, 2005; Marzano & Marzano, 1987, 1989, 2003, 2010).

At the top of figure 1.1 is a box with the phrase *new situation*. New situations can involve people, events, and tasks. This box points to another box titled *working memory*. Inside that box is the term *script*. Working memory is always executing some form of script. The final component of figure 1.1 is titled the *self-system*, which is the system responsible for interpreting a new situation.

The interaction of the components of figure 1.1 illustrates the foundational dynamic of the inner world. At any moment, we are engaged in some type of mental activity. This occurs in our working memory. We examine each new situation that presents itself. Our examination or interpretation of a new situation is conducted within our self-system. This determines what we do or don't do next.

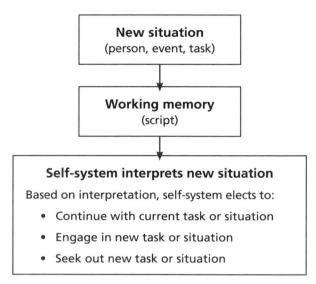

**Figure 1.1: The dynamics of the inner world.**

To illustrate, consider a teacher standing in the front of a classroom presenting information about balancing an equation and demonstrating techniques for doing so. This activity occurs in her working memory (which we discuss in more depth in chapter 4) and is not done extemporaneously. Rather, the teacher is executing a sequence of steps (that is, a script) she typically uses when presenting information and demonstrating procedures.

A script (which we consider in more depth in chapter 2) is a mental structure that defines an appropriate sequence of actions in a particular situation. Human beings have scripts for literally everything they do on a routine basis. The teacher standing at the front of the classroom is executing her script for presenting new content. This script might include elements such as: start by activating students' prior knowledge; next, give students an advance organizer for the new content; then, present the first new piece of information, making sure to keep it short; and so on.

The box below *working memory* reads "Self-system interprets new situation." The self-system (which we consider in more depth in chapter 2) is the repository of all of our goals, needs, and beliefs. It is the mechanism we use to decide what to do and what not to do. Barbara L. McCombs and Robert J. Marzano (1990) noted that the self-system is involved in virtually every decision we make: "the self as agent . . . [is] the basis of will and volition" (p. 66).

The first job of the self-system is to interpret any new situations that come our way. For example, the teacher standing in front of the class might notice a small group of students in the back of the room talking among themselves. This would be a new situation that comes into her consciousness. Up until this point, her working memory was filled with the process (that is, the script) of presenting information, but now something new has caught her attention.

The teacher's self-system would immediately interpret this event. She might interpret the students' actions as a completely inconsequential and anomalous circumstance that will soon dissipate—the students are temporarily distracted and will soon re-engage without her doing anything. In such a case, the teacher would continue executing her script for presenting new information about balancing equations. Alternatively, the teacher might interpret this as a disruption in class. If so, she might stop what she is doing and address this aberrant situation. Stated differently, the teacher would stop executing her "presenting content" script and start executing her "extinguish the interruption" script. This cycle is a basic human dynamic—we continue to execute a script until our interpretation of a new task or situation indicates that we should execute another script.

Figure 1.1 depicts one other possibility regarding what is occurring in working memory at any point in time. When a script is completed, we naturally look for something new to do—a new script to execute. When the teacher completes her "presenting content" script, she will engage in the execution of another script, which will be selected based on goals she has for that particular class. For example, she might have the goal that students engage in some small group work, practicing what she has presented to them. Consequently, the teacher would begin executing her script for setting up such work. When one script reaches its natural end without interruption, we move on to a new script.

## Human Behavior as Mechanistic

Human behavior as depicted in figure 1.1 (page 6) is fairly straightforward—as new situations present themselves to us, we interpret them using our self-systems. Each interpretation carries with it a scripted set of actions. From this perspective, it is easy to conclude that human beings operate in a mechanistic fashion. Indeed, this is an accurate conclusion and, in fact, a positive circumstance for us most of the time. Many of our daily actions are best carried out in a mechanistic way. This has been acknowledged for quite some time. For example, speaking about habitual behavior, Wendy Wood, Jeffrey M. Quinn, and Deborah A. Kashy (2002) noted:

> Habits . . . free people to engage in other kinds of important thoughtful activities such as rumination of past events and planning for future activities. Another important advantage of habits is their association with reduced stress and greater feelings of control. In daily life, habit performance is not likely to deplete self-regulatory resources in the same way as deliberative behavior and this may allow people to conserve regulatory strength for important decisions. (p. 1295)

We could not function well if we thought deeply about performing such actions as tying our shoes, brushing our teeth, taking out the trash, and so on. Mechanistic behavior serves us well during routine tasks. However, mechanistic behavior can lead us astray if we activate a script that is inappropriate or inapplicable to the situation at hand. In fact, reactionary behavior (such as an immediate interpretation that students are misbehaving) might set off a sequence of actions that could turn an inconsequential situation into a major disruption.

Most of us have a number of sad examples of reactionary behavior turning sour. A spouse interprets a trivial comment by her mate as an insult and lashes out at him. A parent interprets a son's arrival after curfew on Saturday night as a challenge of authority and grounds him for a month. These, and more extreme examples we could provide (for example, people who were harmed physically by another person due to a false interpretation of their behavior), place in sharp relief the dangers of mechanistic reactions in certain aspects of our lives. When dealing with other human beings, we must temper our use of scripts with a consideration of our own and others' possible emotions and interpretations. If we do not, mechanistic or impulsive reactions to others' behavior can become hazardous for all concerned. In light of this, teachers are in a precarious situation since they deal with other humans (their students) for some 180 days per year.

In this book, we take the position that teachers can and should be aware of and manage their interpretations of various situations and, when necessary, change their resulting behavior. We refer to this as managing the inner world of teaching.

# Managing the Inner World of Teaching

Managing the inner world of teaching begins with recognizing and acknowledging any situation that elicits strong negative emotions. The reason why strong negative emotions should trigger self-management is addressed in depth in chapter 2. Briefly though, when we have strong negative emotions, we don't think very clearly and tend to adopt a fight-or-flight perspective. When dealing with other people, neither of these two reactions accomplishes much that is positive.

Managing the inner world involves three phases: awareness, analysis, and choice. Each of the three phases has two or more related questions. These are depicted in table 1.2 (page 10).

**Table 1.2: The Three Phases and Their Related Questions**

| Phase | Related Questions |
|---|---|
| Awareness | What emotions am I experiencing right now? |
| | What is my interpretation of this situation? |
| Analysis | What script will I probably execute as the result of my interpretation? |
| | What will be the most probable outcome of my actions? |
| | Will this outcome be the most positive for all concerned? |
| Choice | What is my preferred outcome? |
| | What script do I have to execute to attain this outcome? |

To illustrate how the phases and questions in table 1.2 might manifest, reconsider the teacher who is presenting on balancing equations. As we have noted, at that moment she is executing a script on presenting new content, but she happens to notice students surreptitiously talking among themselves. She notices that she is experiencing negative emotions in response to what she is observing. Instead of reacting immediately, she pauses to ask the first question: What emotions am I experiencing right now? Anger is the first thing that comes to mind, along with the realization that the degree of her anger is increasing rapidly. She considers the second question: What is my interpretation of this situation? It is eminently clear to her that she is interpreting the students' actions as intentionally disrespectful behavior. These first two questions represent the *awareness phase* of managing the inner world—the teacher simply takes some time to be aware of her thinking when she realizes she is upset.

She now switches to a more analytic perspective (the second phase). The third question (What script will I probably execute as the result of my interpretation?) directs her to identify the actions she will most likely take given her interpretation. Given how she feels at that moment, she imagines that she will probably go over to the students and confront them about their behavior. With her level of irritation escalating rapidly, she predicts that she will probably confront students in a manner that lets them know she has become angry. The fourth question is: What will be the most probable outcome of my actions? In answer, she imagines a confrontation that could easily escalate out of control. In answer to the fifth question (Will this outcome be the most positive for all concerned?), she acknowledges that this is something that would not benefit the class as a whole, herself as an individual, or the students who are talking among themselves. This outcome is clearly not something she desires. During the *analysis phase*, the teacher has taken some time to consider the probable consequences of her anticipated actions and whether those consequences are acceptable to her.

The *choice phase* is when the teacher takes responsibility for and exerts control over her behavior. The sixth question, What is my preferred outcome? elicits an image of the students returning their attention to her without being provoked and without further incident. This is much more positive for all concerned. The final question in the sequence is: What script do I have to execute to attain this outcome? She realizes that she will certainly have to walk over to the students and let them know that she would like to regain their attention, but this must be done without appearing angry or drawing undue attention to the incident. She decides to move close to the students and quietly ask them to continue their current conversation after class and refocus their attention on her presentation.

Of course, the seven questions in table 1.2 are stated in formal language to accurately describe their function. In reality, the questions would be addressed quite informally and quickly. The awareness phase might involve asking, "What am I feeling, and why am I feeling this way?" The analysis phase might involve asking, "What will I probably do, what will probably happen, and will this be positive?" The choice phase might include asking, "What do I want to happen, and what do I have to do to make it happen?"

We firmly believe that awareness and control over situations that elicit negative emotions is one of the more powerful skills educators can cultivate to enhance their teaching and provide the most positive and effective learning environment for students. As we shall see, such awareness and control also have the side benefit of enhancing teachers' experience of the classroom and life in general.

## Implications for Teaching

The concept of the inner world of teaching broadens the scope of things teachers should consider as they develop their craft. First, it is important for teachers to be aware of the fact that their experience in the classroom at any point in time is a constructed reality. Moment by moment, teachers are making interpretations about virtually everything that is occurring around them. Based on their interpretations, they react—often without much forethought. Typically, these unexamined reactions are quite appropriate or of little consequence in terms of their effect on students. However, an initial interpretation that generates strong negative emotions can transform a rather inconsequential situation into a major incident. Fortunately, teachers can manage the inner world with awareness, analysis, and choice. These are skills that can and should be practiced by all educators for the good of their students and themselves. The next chapter explores the basic concepts that teachers must understand to effectively manage their inner worlds.

# Chapter 2

## *Understanding the Basics*

The more we understand the workings of the human mind, the more effectively we can manage the inner world. In this chapter, we address four topics that provide a sound basis for understanding and executing the management phases and questions introduced in chapter 1: (1) the power of emotions, (2) the nature of interpretation, (3) scripts, and (4) the importance of the self-system.

## The Power of Emotions

There is a good reason why the first question one asks when managing the inner world is: What emotions am I experiencing right now? It is because emotions are powerful determiners of both thought and behavior. To illustrate the relationship between emotions, thought, and behavior, Jean Piaget (1964) used the analogy of gasoline to an engine. Affect (that is, emotion) is like the gasoline that fuels the engine; affect fuels the process of human thought. Piaget further noted that thought and emotion are inseparable: "There are not two developments, one cognitive and the other affective, two separate psychic functions, nor are there two kinds of objects: all objects are simultaneously cognitive and affective" (p. 39).

Discussions of emotions use various terminologies and have many nuances. Elizabeth A. Linnenbrink (2007) created an organizational tool that classified emotions along two basic dimensions: (1) high activation versus deactivation, and (2) pleasant versus unpleasant. This is depicted in figure 2.1.

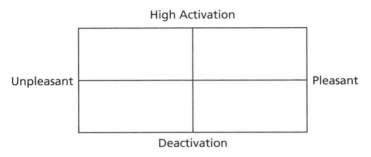

*Source: Adapted from Linnenbrink, 2007.*

**Figure 2.1: The two components of an emotion.**

The vertical axis of figure 2.1 is high activation versus deactivation. *Activation* refers to "arousal, mobilization, and energy" (Linnenbrink, 2007, p. 108). If an emotion is present at the high activation level, it is affecting our thoughts and behavior in a direct way, and we are most probably aware of its presence. If an emotion is deactivated, it is dormant at that point in time. *Pleasant* refers to the positive versus negative valence of an emotion. As we discuss in a subsequent section, all emotions have a biological base, each with its own unique combination of elements. At a very general level, though, emotions fall into two broad categories: positive and negative. Positive emotions generate pleasurable sensations; negative emotions generate unpleasant, even painful, sensations.

As mentioned previously, the names given to the various emotional states we might experience are not standardized. Different people use different terms. For example, Ellen A. Skinner, Thomas A. Kindermann, James P. Connell, and James G. Wellborn (2009) listed the positive versus negative emotions shown in section A of table 2.1, whereas Linnenbrink (2007) listed the positive versus negative emotions shown in section B of table 2.1.

**Table 2.1: Positive Versus Negative Emotions**

| A. Skinner, Kindermann, Connell, and Wellborn (2009) | |
| --- | --- |
| **Positive** | **Negative** |
| Enthusiasm | Boredom |
| Interest | Disinterest |
| Enjoyment | Frustration |
| Satisfaction | Anger |
| Pride | Sadness |
| Vitality | Worry/Anxiety |
| Zest | Shame |
| | Self-Blame |
| **B. Linnenbrink (2007)** | |
| **Positive** | **Negative** |
| Excited | Tense |
| Happy | Angry |
| Relaxed | Sad |
| Calm | Tired |
| | Exhausted |

While the names for the negative and positive emotions listed in table 2.1 are certainly similar, there is still a great deal of variation in the lists. In effect, it appears that there is no universally accepted list or explanation of positive and negative emotions. Here, we focus on a relatively narrow range of emotions with an emphasis on high activation negative ones. We begin with fear.

## Fear Conditioning

For the purpose of managing the inner world, it is important to note that all emotions are not created equal. Negative emotions exert inordinate influence over our thinking and behavior. In fact, the human mind is designed to remember events in our lives that have generated negative emotions—most particularly fear. As Steven M. Southwick and Dennis S. Charney (2012) explained, we tend to remember those events that have generated fear for a specific reason:

> Why does the brain have a mechanism to strengthen memory for dangers and the conditions under which the dangers occur? The answer is survival. An organism that remembers a past danger (through enhanced consolidation) can recognize a similar potential danger in the future, and respond accordingly. Similarly, the organism that remembers the context or stimuli that were associated with a past danger (through fear conditioning) will react to similar stimuli as if a danger is present again. In other words, the neutral stimuli that have been transformed into fear-conditioned stimuli now serve as predictors of potential danger. And, of course, the animal or person that can predict danger is likely to survive and pass on its genes. (p. 49)

The emotion of fear, then, has historically played a strong, positive role in our survival. We must learn from situations that are dangerous or threatening so that we avoid similar situations in the future. The fear we sometimes experience with our interpretations is a protective mechanism to help us more accurately predict future threats. Joseph E. LeDoux (2002) explained further:

> If an animal is lucky enough to survive one dangerous encounter, its brain should store as much about the experience as possible, and this learning should not decay over time, since a predator will always be a predator. In modern life, we sometimes suffer from the exquisite operation of this system, since it is difficult to get rid of this kind of conditioning once it is no longer applicable to our lives, and we sometimes become conditioned to fear things that are in fact harmless. Evolution's wisdom sometimes comes at a cost. (p. 124)

LeDoux's comments describe the unintended consequences of our biological tendency to accentuate the events that generate fear in us. Simply stated, few things in modern life that activate fear conditioning are true threats to our survival. Consequently, our tendency to more readily remember events in our lives associated with fear may generally be more of a liability than an asset.

## Fight-or-Flight Thinking

Fear conditioning not only helps us remember the situations we perceive as threats, it also distorts our thinking in the short term. This is due to the fight-or-flight response. Southwick and Charney (2012) explained that the fight-or-flight response was first described by Harvard physiologist Walter B. Cannon in the early 20th century. Cannon (1927) contended that without any conscious effort on our part, our body prepares itself for one of two responses to any situation that is perceived as a threat: fight or flight. There is no volition involved; once we perceive a threat, that threat elicits a chemical response. As Southwick and Charney explained:

> The fight-flight response is mediated, in part, by a group of chemicals called catecholamines (which include epinephrine, norepinephrine, and dopamine). These chemicals are released by the nervous system in response to perceived danger. Catecholamines shut down blood flow to the digestive system, which slows during dangerous situations, and instead shunt blood to the heart and skeletal muscles, which are needed for fighting or fleeing. Our reflexes sharpen and blood flow to capillaries decreases. This reduces bleeding if we are wounded. (p. 46)

Drawing from the work of Barbara L. Fredrickson (2001), Southwick and Charney (2012) explained that the fight-or-flight "reaction narrows our visual focus and tends to restrict our behaviors to those that are essential for attacking or fleeing" (p. 32). While the laser-like focus generated by the fight-or-flight response is useful when faced with imminent physical danger, it is not useful in situations where it is beneficial to consider multiple options regarding a situation (Finucane, 2011).

In effect, fear activates chemicals called catecholamines, the ultimate effect of which is to focus our attention. But this also inhibits our ability to consider a wide array of behaviors. Interestingly, positive emotions have the opposite effect:

> Positive emotions, in contrast, have been shown to reduce physiological arousal and to broaden our visual focus, our thoughts, and our behavior. When people experience positive emotions and an accompanying broadening of attention and behavior, their thinking tends to become more creative, inclusive, flexible, and integrative. (Southwick & Charney, 2012, p. 32)

The differential effects of positive versus negative emotions have been reported by many (see Fredrickson, 1998; Gable & Harmon-Jones, 2011; Zivot, Cohen, & Kapucu, 2013). The fact that negative emotions narrow our frame of reference whereas positive emotions broaden our frame of reference is of no small consequence. Every time we become fearful, angry, disgusted, or unhappy (or any of the other names used to label the activation of catecholamines), we become less capable of thinking rationally. We interpret our environment through a very narrow filter that was useful to the prehistoric human facing the saber-toothed tiger but not to the teacher facing a small group of misbehaving students.

## Anger

Anger is a close cousin of fear and is worthy of consideration on its own. In her book *Anger: The Misunderstood Emotion*, Carol Tavris (1989) identified common myths about anger. These myths are briefly described in table 2.2. Coupling the listing of myths in table 2.2 with the previous discussion of the fight-or-flight response provides for an interesting perspective on anger. One can make a case that anger begets anger. It doesn't dissipate once expressed. Rather, once acted on, anger generates a negative spiral that is continually more and more focused on what we perceive to be its source.

**Table 2.2: Myths About Anger**

| Myth | Reality |
|------|---------|
| **Aggression Is the Instinctive Catharsis for Anger.** | Aggression is a learned response to anger. Different cultures teach different ways to express anger. Even across cultures, females are typically not taught to express anger through aggression. |
| **Talking Out Anger Gets Rid of It—or at Least Makes You Feel Less Angry.** | Talking about what has made you angry tends to reactivate the original anger you felt and increase the probability that you will react angrily in similar situations. |
| **Tantrums and Other Childhood Rages Are Healthy Expressions of Anger That Forestall Neurosis.** | A tantrum is not a natural expression of anger in children. Rather, it is a response children learn when it produces some form of desired effect. Allowing young children to have tantrums increases the probability that they will continue to have them long after the point at which they would have naturally died out due to social pressure. |

*Source: Tavris, 1989.*

One of the more sobering aspects of anger is that our environment can prime us to outbursts of anger by subtle and not-so-subtle stimuli in our lives. Tavris (1989) explained the phenomenon from the perspective of epinephrine and norepinephrine, two of the catecholamines associated with strong negative emotions:

> The list of things now known to cause a rise in these two hormones reads like a catalog of modern life: heat, cold, pain . . . hypoglycemia, low blood pressure (hypotension), hemorrhage, burns, physical exercise; drugs such as caffeine, nicotine, and alcohol; and "psychosocial stimuli," or what people do to you—an unexpected elbow in the ribs, an insult from a stranger or spouse, a dashing of your hopes

for a promotion. Epinephrine rises not only in response to overstimulation, but also from understimulation. The body must cope with the exhilaration of a walk through a high-density, complex, strange new city, and it must cope with the boredom of repetitive, tedious chores. . . . Epinephrine and norepinephrine are what provide the *feeling* of a feeling: that tingle, arousal, excitement, energy. The adrenal hormones act on all organs of the body reached by the sympathetic nervous system, stimulating the heart, dilating coronary vessels, constricting blood vessels in the intestines, and shutting off digestion. (p. 89)

Tavris's description of those factors that predispose us to anger is as frightening as it is informative and useful. As we go through our daily lives, little events as inconsequential as being jostled on the bus, or being overtired, or being in some physical discomfort, increase our levels of epinephrine and norepinephrine, pushing us to the threshold of anger. It is no wonder, then, that a harried and pressured teacher might overreact to a group of students perceived as being disrespectful.

In her final analysis, Tavris (1989) offered the following advice regarding anger:

The moral of this story is: When you feel provoked, count to ten; and when you are also hot, hungry, exercising, walking along a noisy street, booing the opposition in a crowded stadium, driving a car to (or from) work, or disturbed for the forty-fifth time when you have a deadline tomorrow, count to a hundred. The world being what it is, most of us do not realize how often we are agitated by the background stimulants of our lives. There is usually a lag between the source of arousal and a provocation, and the longer the lag, the greater the ambiguity of explanation. As research shows, when you have a choice between interpretations ("That anger must be my tension speaking" versus "Cynthia is truly obnoxious"), you are likely to choose the human provocation over the physical state. But when you know that your levels of epinephrine will jump sharply because of noise, heat, exercise, hunger, frustration, or crowds, you are better able to interpret your bodily sensations and are less susceptible to provocation than are people who do not know why they feel so jumpy. Knowledge is power—in this case, to decide whether you need a quiet evening alone or a discussion with Cynthia. And it suggests that, should you decide on the latter, you don't do it in the cooling-down room after a vigorous tennis game, or you may heat up the argument. (pp. 191–192)

Tavris's suggestion references the well-used adage of "count to ten" when you become angry. But Tavris goes much further, explaining that we should monitor our state of equilibrium versus disequilibrium in a systematic way to determine if we are in a heightened state of arousal. A brief pause for reflection and calming can stave off the increased potential for angry outbursts. Hence, the need for the first question addressed when managing the inner world: What emotions am I experiencing right now? If those emotions are negative, start counting. Finally, Tavris introduces a very powerful management tool—controlling our interpretations of new situations.

# The Nature of Interpretation

The second question addressed when managing the inner world is: What is my interpretation of this situation? We saw in chapter 1 that human beings interpret virtually every new situation that presents itself—the students talking in the back of the room, the student smiling at us in the front of the room, a frown on the face of an acquaintance, the lack of a response to a telephone call we made, and so on. Interpretation is at the core of human thought. John O'Shaughnessy (2009) explained:

Interpretation is basic to all our endeavors whether as scientists or as individuals going about our daily lives. . . . Every time we deliberate on events or on our experience, we are interpreting. Interpretation is fundamental since how things are interpreted determines what actions we consider. (p. 1)

Interpretation can be described as the process of assigning a new situation to a category. A student sitting in the front row smiles at us. We interpret this as an example of the category "a student being friendly or attentive." A student turns away from us when we smile at him. We interpret this as an example of the category "a student being annoyed." Fundamentally, when presented with new situations, we ask and answer the question, What is this an example of? Every situation is relegated to a category.

It is probably safe to say that it is difficult, if not impossible, to desist from categorizing. Albert Einstein (1949/1970) noted that "thinking without the positing of categories and of concepts in general would be as impossible as is breathing in a vacuum" (p. 674). The process is so innate that it occurs unnoticed, below our level of consciousness.

## How We Create Categories

We form categories in two basic ways: (1) we learn them from other people, and (2) we create them from our own observations. Learning categories from other people starts at a very early age. We hear or see our parents categorizing various people, events, and tasks, and we tend to incorporate their categories into our own view of the world. Of course, we can pick up biases and stereotypes through this process; we assume that people, events, or tasks within a specific category all possess the same characteristics. For example, as children we hear one of our parents make a comment that people with beards tend to have certain characteristics. We then incorporate this category of "people with beards" into our thinking. As adolescents, we hear our friends make comments about people who dress a certain way possessing specific characteristics. This too becomes a category we use to interpret the situations presented to us.

Research suggests that the influence of the expressed beliefs and opinions of those we encounter as children is strong and expansive. In 1954, Gordon W. Allport wrote that "the home influence has priority, and that the child has excellent reasons for adopting his ethnic attitudes ready-made from his parents. . . . Up to [puberty] . . . a child's prejudices are mostly secondhand" (pp. 297, 312). In 2013, Juliane Degner and Jonas Dalege conducted a meta-analysis to examine similarities between parents' and their children's attitudes toward other social groups. They found a significant positive relationship between parents' attitudes and children's attitudes toward particular groups. Regarding the influence of nonparental factors on children's categorizations of different groups of people, Degner and Dalege observed that "internal and external sources interactively and reciprocally enforce the construction of links of social categories with attributes" (p. 1272), and Martyn Barrett (2007) emphasized that children can form categories based on information they encounter during interactions with their parents, teachers, peer groups, textbooks, media, television, books, and the Internet, although parents are considered to be particularly influential.

The second way we form categories is from our own observations. This is basically a process of induction. John H. Holland, Keith J. Holyoak, Richard E. Nisbett, and Paul R. Thagard (1986) postulated rules of induction that allow us to form categories. Some of those rules are briefly described in table 2.3 (page 24). Once formed, categories created by observation and induction are the same as categories we have learned from other people. They can contain rules and generalizations that are accurate and inaccurate. Observation and induction are no guarantee against bias or prejudice.

## Generalizing

Once we have formed categories for people, events, and tasks (whether they be learned categories or induced categories), we use them to draw conclusions about the situations we encounter. This is commonly referred to as *generalizing*. Charles G. Lord and Cheryl A. Taylor (2009) explained that "people so readily generalize that they often 'know' in advance what they are going to like and what they are going to dislike. They develop assumptions and expectations, which in part determine their future evaluative responses" (p. 827).

It is the process of generalizing that generates our expectations about any person, event, or task that we encounter. We interpret a specific student as a member of the "underachiever" category; we then

**Table 2.3: Three Rules of Induction**

| Rule | Description |
|------|-------------|
| **Rule of Large Numbers** | This rule states that when we infer a rule or generalization about a category of people, events, or tasks, then we assume that the rule or characteristic applies to all members of the category. However, we also attach a strength or likelihood parameter to the rule or generalization based on how many elements we have observed. For example, you move to a new school and observe that many of the teachers in the school gather on Friday after school at a local restaurant. You form a rule that states that teachers in this type of school value social interaction. However, you also note that the rule is not absolute because some teachers seem to avoid the "Friday-afternoon club" activities. |
| **Regulation Rule** | This rule states that if we infer a rule or generalization about a category of people, events, or tasks that takes the form, *If you want to do x with an element of this category, then you must first do y*, then you should also create a related rule of the form, *If you do not do y, then you cannot do x*. For example, as a new member of the faculty in a school, you have induced the rule that if you want to receive help from the teachers in your department, then you must become part of their social network. Given this rule, you form a related one, which might be: If you are not willing to become part of the social network, then don't expect any help. |
| **Unusualness Rule** | This rule states that if an unexpected property is observed regarding a rule or generalization for a category of people, events, or tasks, then amend the rule or generalization to specify the conditions under which the unexpected property might occur. For example, if you happen to receive help from a teacher outside of your department, then you amend your rule about receiving help only if you are part of the social network to apply only to your department. |

assume that the student possesses every characteristic and behavior that we associate with underachievers. We interpret parent-teacher conferences as a member of the "rituals that have little or no effect on student learning" category; we then assume that this activity has all the characteristics and follows all the rules regarding such events.

Knowing that our interpretations come from our categories and that our categories are used to generalize can help us guard against habitual behavior that might not be useful in specific situations. Habitual behaviors are referred to as scripts.

## Scripts

The third question relative to managing the inner world addresses the script we will most probably execute given our interpretation. Holland and his colleagues (1986) posited that along with rules and characteristics associated with a category, we generate a list of actions we should perform when confronted with an element of a category. For example, when we encounter a dog that falls into the category of "aggressive animal," we activate specific actions—in this case, such actions might include: talking in a calm, soothing voice; slowly backing away; moving to the other side of the street; and so on. When we encounter a student who falls into the category of "difficult to control," we activate specific actions, which might include: look the student right in the eyes; don't smile; speak deliberately; move close to the student; and so on. Once we have categorized a person, event, or task, we then know how we will interact with that person, event, or task.

The concept of scripts was made popular by Roger C. Schank and Robert Abelson (1977), both from the field of artificial intelligence. They define scripts in the following way:

> A script is a structure that describes appropriate sequences of events in a particular context. A script is made up of slots and requirements about what can fill those slots. The structure is an interconnected whole, and what is in one slot affects

what can be in another. Scripts handle stylized everyday situations. They are not subject to much change, nor do they provide the apparatus for handling totally novel situations. Thus, a script is a predetermined, stereotyped sequence of actions that defines a well-known situation. (p. 41)

Teun van Dijk (1980) further explained that scripts have prototypical components (those that are always executed when engaged in a specific activity) and free components (those that might be executed in a specific situation but are not necessary to accomplish the task at hand). For example, our script for getting ready to go to work might have the prototypical components of getting up by a certain time, getting dressed within a specific interval of time, getting to the bus stop by a certain time, and so on. These components are necessary to successfully complete the task. Free components might be actions such as having a cup of coffee to drink right after taking a shower, watching the early news program on the local channel while getting dressed, and so on. These free components aren't necessary to complete the task but are actions that we like to engage in if time allows.

Schank and Abelson (1977) dramatized the nature of scripts using the "restaurant" script. It is depicted in table 2.4. Table 2.4 lists the prototypical components (those that will always be executed) when frequenting a restaurant—we enter the restaurant, find a suitable table or are escorted to a table by a server, we examine the menu, and so on. Free components for the "restaurant" script might include having a short but pleasant conversation with the server, taking a few moments to relax and look around before looking at the menu, and so on.

Scripts are ubiquitous in our lives. In fact, we probably have tens of thousands of them; we need scripts to operate in an efficient manner. Most scripts have little or no potential to cause harm. However, scripts that involve people, events, or tasks to which we are reacting negatively can be quite destructive. Recall the discussion of the fight-or-flight response when we experience fear. If we have assigned a person, event, or task to a category that we perceive as threatening, we will execute a "fight" script or a "flight" script. "Fight" scripts commonly activate fear's close cousin, anger.

**Table 2.4: The "Restaurant" Script**

| | |
|---|---|
| **Roles** | Customer, waitress, chef, cashier |
| **Reason** | To get food so as to go up in pleasure and down in hunger |
| **Scene 1: Entering** | • Enter restaurant<br>• Find empty table<br>• Sit at empty table |
| **Scene 2: Ordering** | • Receive menu<br>• Read menu<br>• Decide what to eat<br>• Give order to server |
| **Scene 3: Eating** | • Receive food<br>• Eat food<br>• Engage in pleasant conversation while eating if accompanied by others |
| **Scene 4: Exiting** | • Ask for check<br>• Receive check<br>• Pay check and tip server<br>• Leave restaurant |

In their book *Fighting for Your Marriage*, Howard J. Markman, Scott M. Stanley, and Susan L. Blumberg (2010) dramatically illustrated the destructive consequences of executing a "fight" script with a spouse. A husband categorizes an action by his wife as an example of a disrespectful behavior. He executes a "fight" script designed to extinguish his wife's behavior at that moment and in the future. Unfortunately, his wife interprets his behavior as an action that warrants the execution of her own "fight" script designed to extinguish her husband's behavior. The session escalates into a situation that is harmful to both parties. The same dynamic can occur in the classroom. We interpret a student's actions in a way that elicits a "fight" script from us, which in turn elicits a "fight" script from the student. No one wins, and both parties are negatively affected by the episode.

# The Importance of the Self-System

In chapter 1, we briefly addressed the seminal role of the self-system in directing our behavior. It is difficult to ascribe too much importance to the self-system since it literally affects all aspects of our lives. Mihaly Csikszentmihalyi (1990) described the self-system in the following way:

> The self is no ordinary piece of information. . . . It contains everything . . . that has passed through consciousness: all the memories, actions, desires, pleasures, and pains are included in it. And more than anything else, the self represents the hierarchy of goals that we have built up, bit by bit, over the years. . . . At any given time, we are usually aware of only a tiny part of it. (p. 34)

The basic structure of the self-system can be described as a hierarchy of goals or desired states. Sometimes these goals and desired states are referred to as *needs*. There have been a number of attempts to identify the types of goals and desired states that constitute the self-system (see Adams, 1963, 1965; Alderfer, 1969; Deci & Ryan, 1985; Herzberg, Mausner, & Snyderman, 1967; McClelland, 1965; Skinner, 1938, 1953; Vroom, 1964). The model we use here is an adaptation of a well-known system created by Abraham Maslow (1943, 1954).

Maslow's original hierarchy contained five levels: physiology, safety, belonging, self-esteem, and self-actualization. We have added a sixth level—connection to something greater than the self. Table 2.5 depicts our adaptation and expansion of Maslow's hierarchy.

## Table 2.5: Adaptation and Expansion of Maslow's Hierarchy

| Level | Goals or Desired States |
|---|---|
| 6: Connection to Something Greater Than Self | Experiencing life as meaningful and purposeful |
| 5: Self-Actualization | Recognizing the desire for personal accomplishments; working toward and completing these accomplishments |
| 4: Esteem Within a Community | Experiencing admiration and respect from your peers |
| 3: Belonging Within a Community | Experiencing your peers as welcoming your involvement with them |
| 2: Physical Safety | Experiencing your immediate environment as devoid of physical threat |
| 1: Physiological Comfort | Experiencing your immediate environment as meeting threshold levels of need regarding temperature, sustenance, light, and general comfort |

The goals and desired states on the right side of table 2.5 are the basic filters we use to interpret new situations. Fundamentally, if we interpret a new situation as a challenge or impediment to a goal or desired state at any level, we react negatively. Of course, such an interpretation elicits negative emotions, which elicit scripts designed to protect us. Conversely, if we interpret a situation as facilitating or supporting a goal or desired state, we embrace it and execute a script designed to take advantage of the current situation.

To illustrate, consider the physiological need for a comfortable temperature. If we are in a room where it is too cold, we will seek to decrease the heat loss from our body by doing something like putting on a coat or a sweater. At the level of safety, we will move to the far side of a busy street that has no sidewalk to lessen the chances of being hit by a speeding car. Regarding the goal or desired state of belonging, we will seek out groups of people who have interests similar to our own, such as the same type of preferred recreational activities. Relative to the goal or desired state of esteem, we will try to master those skills important to our selected form of recreation to be seen as highly competent among the other members of that group. With respect to self-actualization, we will seek to become knowledgeable about a topic like gardening if we personally consider that as a domain of importance. Concerning connection to something greater than self, we will seek out and spend substantial time and energy on a cause we believe benefits our community or the world in general, even if it does not tangibly benefit our personal lives.

Our needs drive the way we view the world. In effect, we are always scanning our environment from the perspective of the right side of table 2.5. We are continually asking ourselves questions like:

- Is this situation comfortable from a physiological perspective? (level 1)
- Is this situation safe? (level 2)
- Am I welcome in this situation? (level 3)
- Do I have a sense of status in this situation? (level 4)
- Does this situation allow me to move toward a personal goal? (level 5)
- Does this situation provide an opportunity to better things around me? (level 6)

Our natural human tendency is to work toward positive answers to these questions. This tendency is ubiquitous in nature and is described in cybernetic theory. *Cybernetics* is the "field of control and communication theory" (Wiener, 1961, p. 11) which is "concerned with the study of systems of any nature which are capable of receiving, storing, and processing information so as to use it for control" (Kolmogorov, n.d.). Cybernetic theory is the basis for many machines we use on a daily basis. The most obvious example is a thermostat. The temperature we select for the thermostat is the desired state. The thermostat continually monitors the ambient temperature, comparing it to the desired state. When the ambient temperature is lower than the desired state, the furnace is activated. When the ambient temperature is higher than the desired state, the air conditioner is activated.

For decades, cybernetic theory has also been used to explain human behavior. For example, in a series of works, William Glasser (1965, 1969, 1981) detailed how humans are constantly attempting to make the outside world match their internal expectations. This goes a long way toward explaining our propensity to react in mechanistic ways. Our self-systems are designed for survival. All of us are—at any point in time—trying to control our environment to meet our goals and desired states. By definition, this creates self-serving behaviors except at the sixth level of the hierarchy— connection to something greater than self. As we discuss in chapter 5, when we operate from this level, our focus is on altruistic behavior.

It is useful to keep the dynamics of the self-system in mind when dealing with students who might annoy us. They are simply trying to survive in a world that frequently looks like a threat to many of their goals and desired states.

Finally, an understanding of the self-system highlights the importance of operating from the sixth level of the hierarchy as much as possible in our roles as teachers. Thinking of the good of others (most pointedly, our students) when we make decisions about how to act is always a wise move. It not only helps those in our care but also affords us the opportunity to operate at our highest level of goals and desired states.

# Implications for Teaching

The four topics addressed in this chapter all have direct implications for teaching. The power of emotions—particularly negative ones—to influence human thinking should be an awareness every teacher cultivates. Indeed, the power of negative emotions to affect our ability to make rational decisions is precisely why the first question asked while managing the inner world is, What emotions am I experiencing right now?

The second management question is, What is my interpretation of this situation? The fact that our interpretations are based on characteristics of a category that we generalize to specific people, events, and tasks we encounter should provide a cautionary note regarding our initial thinking. Our conclusions might be accurate about the situation at hand, or they might be inaccurate. Awareness of a current interpretation in terms of its accuracy can be a powerful tool in manipulating and controlling our behavior.

The concept of scripts is fundamental to the third question of the management sequence: What script will I probably execute as the result of my interpretation? It is also fundamental to the fourth question: What will be the most probable outcome of my actions? A consideration of the consequences of our actions based on the script we will execute again puts us in direct control over our actions.

The hierarchy of goals and desired states of the self-system provides insight into the fifth, sixth, and seventh management questions: Will this outcome be the most positive for all concerned? What is my preferred outcome? What script do I have to execute to attain this outcome? Specifically, these questions allow us to consider the potential effects of our actions on the various levels of needs and desired states within our own self-system and the self-systems of those who will be affected by our actions and select alternative scripts that will help us operate at our highest level of goals and desired states. In the next chapter, we turn our attention to ways that teachers can practice using the management sequence to improve their interactions with students.

# Chapter 3

## *Practicing Management of the Inner World*

Managing the inner world is a skill that requires deliberate practice over an extended period of time. We can garner such practice in a variety of ways including retrospective practice, mental rehearsal, and real-time practice. We begin with retrospective practice.

## Retrospective Practice

To practice managing the inner world retrospectively, we begin by identifying situations that typically elicit strong negative emotions. Up until this point, we have used the term *situations* in a relatively loose manner. Here, we note that there are three types of situations we should consider when engaging in retrospective practice: people, events, and tasks.

### Retrospective Practice Regarding People

To illustrate retrospective practice regarding people at school, consider a teacher who retrospectively thinks about the students in her class. She begins by asking herself which of her students typically elicits a negative emotional response. She realizes that she experiences anger when she interacts with one student, Maria. It isn't the type of anger that makes her want to lash out at Maria. Rather, it is a mild but recurring feeling of irritation that colors all interactions with her. The second question the teacher asks focuses on her interpretation of Maria. In response to this focus, the teacher realizes she usually interprets Maria's behavior as disrespectful to her. On further consideration, the teacher realizes that this interpretation challenges her own sense of self-esteem; if Maria does not respect her, are there other students who feel the same way? This represents the awareness phase of the management process. She is now cognizant of her reaction to Maria.

The third question requires the teacher to consider the script she typically executes when interacting with Maria. She realizes that she ignores Maria during class. Specifically, she doesn't make eye contact with Maria; she doesn't even get in close physical proximity to her. If she doesn't have to interact with Maria, she doesn't think about the challenges to her self-esteem. She next asks herself about the most probable outcome of the typical way she interacts with Maria. A little thought leads her to the realization that her actions don't help her feel any better about Maria and most probably don't help Maria feel any better about her. In fact, her actions are probably making Maria feel more and more alienated. Given this, the answer to the next management question is easy to discern: Will this outcome be the most positive for all concerned? Clearly, the teacher would rather that Maria and she both have interactions that bring them closer together as opposed to further apart. These three considerations represent the analysis phase of the management process.

The choice phase of the process provides the teacher with the opportunity to change the predictable outcome of her interactions with Maria. It begins with the question: What is my preferred outcome? The teacher realizes that she would like to start by changing her feelings about Maria. Instead of experiencing irritation, she would rather leave interactions with Maria with a sense of improved understanding of her. The final management question—What script do I have to execute to attain this outcome?—requires the teacher to come up with a new plan of action or script for dealing with Maria. This gives the teacher pause because it requires her to think of new ways of interacting. She starts by making a commitment to have more personal contact with Maria, talking to her and standing near her more frequently. She realizes that over time she will add more details to this new and burgeoning script, but for now she has identified a good starting place.

## Retrospective Practice Regarding Events

To illustrate retrospective practice regarding events, consider a teacher who examines his response to the event of passing periods in the hallway. He works in a large urban high school with many students who come from backgrounds of poverty, quite unlike his advantaged background. One of the events he likes the least is passing periods between classes, particularly when he happens to be in the hallway. He picks this event to analyze.

He begins by asking himself, "What emotions do I experience during passing periods?" He quickly realizes that it is a subtle form of fear and the sense that things are out of control. He was already aware of the fact that he did not like passing periods, but the realization that he experiences fear is new to him. Next he asks, "How do I typically interpret passing periods?" The more he thinks about the question, the more he realizes that he interprets them as something dangerous, even at a physical level—a fight might break out, which he will be expected to handle. Again, this gives him pause.

He next asks, "What script do I typically execute during passing periods?" To his great surprise, he realizes that he becomes aggressive—frowning at students, standing somewhat defiantly in the middle of the hallway, subtly looking for students to challenge him. The realizations he experiences from these questions provide him with an awareness he never had before—hallway passing periods disturb him greatly. He next considers the outcomes that typically arise from his actions. He concludes that the vast majority of students don't react to his aggressive demeanor. Most simply walk by him without making eye contact. However, given that he is "looking for trouble" in the hallway, he sometimes finds it. He thinks back on a few instances when a simple glance from a student elicited a comment from him ("Do you have a problem, Michael?") that in turn sparked an even more negative reaction in the student. In answer to the next question (Is this outcome the most positive for all concerned?), his answer is an unqualified no. His analysis of the situation has put the need for change in sharp relief.

During the choice phase, he stops to consider what type of outcome he would prefer. Upon reflection, he concludes that he would like his presence to have a calming effect on students during passing time, as opposed to an inflammatory effect. He realizes that to make this happen, he must stop his aggressive actions and be friendlier as students pass by. The final question he addresses is, What script do I have to execute to attain this outcome? The answer to this question represents new territory for him, and he realizes that he will have to seek information on such types of behavior. How do you act calm and supportive when you are nervous and fearful? He makes a commitment to finding new patterns of behavior that are more helpful to students.

## Retrospective Practice Regarding Tasks

To illustrate retrospective practice regarding tasks, consider a middle school teacher who has the task of monitoring study hall. She asks herself, "What is my emotional response when I am charged with monitoring study hall?" She realizes she is both irritated and bored when it is her duty. She has been aware of this for quite some time. The second question (What is my interpretation of this task?) helps her discover why she experiences irritation and boredom. It's because she considers this activity a waste of time both for herself and her students.

When she asks about the script she typically executes during this task as a result of her interpretation, she realizes that while monitoring study hall, she doesn't do anything she considers productive. She simply observes students and tends to daydream. By the end of her monitoring duty, she has accomplished nothing of personal importance. The next question focuses on the probable outcomes of her actions; she quickly realizes that her actions are a setup for her not to accomplish anything useful. She basically goes into a "pause mode" during this task. This makes the answer to the next question (Is this outcome the most positive for all concerned?) quite obvious—no.

When she considers a more preferable outcome, she realizes that she would like to complete her study hall duty with the sense that she has made progress on something or accomplished something; the more she thinks about this, the more she comes to the conclusion that she would like to feel that students have been positively influenced by her presence as study hall supervisor. When she considers the actions or script she must execute to attain the new outcome, she soon begins to craft a list of things she will do, such as identify students who are having difficulty and offer to help them, get to know some of the students better, and the like.

# Preparing for the Day

To heighten awareness of potential situations we might encounter that require management, it is useful to begin each day with a consideration of the potential people, events, and tasks we might encounter. This could be done first thing in the morning, perhaps while driving to work. For example, a teacher might conduct a quick mental audit of the students in each of her classes, taking her "emotional temperature" as she does so. For the first period, she notes that she is a bit annoyed at Alexandra because of her unwillingness to participate in class. Second-period students raise no red flags relative to her emotional reactions, but third period affords her a strong reaction. She notices that two students, Jay and Mark, elicit a fairly strong sense of anger. They have recently behaved in a manner that she thinks is contrived to annoy her. She is a bit surprised at the strength and negativity of her reaction. Students in the rest of her class periods do not elicit any noticeable negative responses. The teacher also does a quick mental scan of the tasks and events that she may encounter throughout the day. She notices that the task of monitoring the cafeteria creates a reaction of anxiety.

In most situations, simply being aware of those people, events, and tasks that stir emotions in us is enough preparation to ensure that we don't react by executing a script that is not beneficial to us or others. However, in some situations, we might find it useful to examine why a person, event, or task generated such a response. This is tantamount to asking the second question of the management process: What is my interpretation of this situation? The teacher who has identified the two students in her third period class who are problematic has already articulated her interpretation when she acknowledges that she believes their actions are contrived to bother her. This conclusion, of course, is an interpretation that will most likely elicit a script on her part that is harmful or at least not very productive. With this awareness, the teacher might briefly think of another interpretation that is less bothersome to her. (For example, the students have not targeted her. Rather, they are simply at an age where they like to test the limits that have been placed on them.)

In an extreme case, a teacher might even want to engage in some mental rehearsal. At a very basic level, mental rehearsal involves visualizing ourselves engaged in some action we will execute. In effect, we can use mental rehearsal to practice a script we would like to perfect. Robert J. Marzano and Tammy Heflebower (2012) explained that the concept of mental rehearsal has a rich history in the world of sports. They provided the following example of Sylvie Bernier, an Olympic diving champion who used mental rehearsal to practice each of her dives:

> I did my dives in my head all the time. At night, before going to sleep, I always did my dives. Ten dives. I started with a front dive, the first one that I had to do at the Olympics, and I did everything as if I was actually there. I saw myself in the pool at the Olympics doing my dives. If the dive was wrong, I went back and started over. For me it was better than a workout. I felt like I was on the board. (as cited in Orlick, 2008, p. 105)

The effectiveness of mental rehearsal is not limited to physical skills. Rather, it can also be used to practice metacognitive skills such as managing the inner world of teaching. To illustrate how mental rehearsal might be used to this end, consider the teacher who has interpreted the actions of two of her third-period students as a conscious attempt on their part to annoy her. She already realizes that this is an interpretation that is not necessarily true. She has even selected an alternative interpretation that is more acceptable to her—they are simply at an age where they are testing the limits imposed by adults in their lives. Sometime prior to class, she takes a few moments to imagine herself observing the students from the front of the class. She sees their typical giggly behavior that bothers her. She next imagines that their behavior has little or no effect on her. Instead of letting herself get upset, she calmly executes a script in which she asks the students to return their attention to class. This brief mental rehearsal provides her with a new script for her next encounter with the two students.

# Managing the Inner World in Real Time

The management process is meant to be executed on a moment-by-moment, real-time basis throughout the day. Its purpose, of course, is to stop negative emotions from triggering scripts that worsen a potentially harmful situation. This does not mean that we must be conscious of our thoughts at all times. Indeed, this would be distracting and counterproductive. However, it does mean that we must be aware of strong negative emotional reactions as they occur.

If a situation evokes such a response, then we take some time to think before we act. We can address the three phases quite quickly. During the awareness phase, we consider our emotional response and our interpretation of the present situation. During the analysis phase, we consider our probable actions, the outcome of those actions, and whether the outcome is beneficial to us and others. During the choice phase, we identify the outcome we would prefer and the actions we will have to take to effect the desired outcome. All of this can occur in a very brief period of time. In chapter 1, we presented the following more "streamlined" set of management questions:

**Awareness Phase**—What am I feeling, and why am I feeling this way?

**Analysis Phase**—What will I probably do, what will probably happen, and will this be positive?

**Choice Phase**—What do I want to happen, and what do I have to do to make it happen?

The following vignette depicts how a teacher might quickly engage in the awareness, analysis, and choice phases of the management process in real time.

*Ms. Cameron, a third-grade teacher, is working with a small group of students during a math lesson one day. As she scans the rest of the class working independently, she notices a disturbance at Jamison's desk. Throughout the year, Jamison has struggled during independent work times, often engaging in off-task behavior and distracting other students in the process. Today, instead of working on his seatwork, Jamison has decided to draw cartoons of his classmates in his math notebook and show them to his neighbors. The students around Jamison are laughing, and the rest of the class has begun to notice and become curious. Almost immediately, Ms. Cameron notices her own negative emotional response to the situation. Taking some time to ask herself what emotions she is experiencing and what her interpretation of the situation is, she recognizes that she feels angry and interprets the situation as a threat to the orderliness and productivity of her classroom. Moving to the analysis phase, she recognizes that probable actions in response to the disturbance include saying Jamison's name, walking to his desk, reprimanding him for his off-task behavior, making him apologize to the rest of the class for his choices, and taking away his recess time for the rest of the week. Having taken these actions before, she is able to predict their outcomes fairly easily. Jamison will probably sulkily apologize to the class, she will have to supervise him during recess time for the rest of the week, and she will likely get a call from his mother about his recess being taken away. Ms. Cameron unhesitatingly decides that these outcomes are not the most positive for all concerned. Transitioning to the choice phase, Ms. Cameron decides that her preferred outcome is for Jamison and the rest of the class to return to their independent work, while communicating to Jamison that she cares about him but doesn't approve of the choices he is currently making. To achieve these outcomes, Ms. Cameron decides on a new set of actions to execute instead. Quietly asking her small group to excuse her for a moment, she walks to Jamison's desk, kneels down next to him, and asks for his help. She says, "I know you love to draw, and I would like to talk about what you've drawn, but right now, the class needs to focus on their seatwork. What can you do to help that happen?" Jamison, surprised at Ms. Cameron's kind manner, replies that he could focus on his own work and not distract other students. Ms. Cameron affirms that Jamison's choice would be a great one and lets him know she'll come back in a few minutes to see how his work is going. She does, and Jamison has made progress on his math task. Later that day, Ms. Cameron meets privately with Jamison to talk about his drawing and discuss the inappropriateness of drawing cartoons of other students in class.*

# Managing Volatile Situations

We must provide one caution regarding the process of managing the inner world. It is important to note that sometimes a strong emotional response signals actual danger and should be acted on, as opposed to examined. For example, if a student threatens us, we will most probably have an emotional response of fear. Instead of thinking about our fear reaction, we should move to extinguish the danger quickly and deliberately. We recommend that all teachers develop one or more scripts they have practiced and can execute when a situation is truly dangerous. In particular, we recommend the script summarized in table 3.1 (pages 42–43).

**Table 3.1: Recommended Plan for Defusing Dangerous Situations**

| Step | Action (Scripts) |
|---|---|
| **1. Know Your Students' Tendencies.** | In many cases, previous instances of aggressive behavior are the best predictors of future incidents. Thus, it is important for teachers to be aware of students who have exhibited aggressive behaviors or angry outbursts in the past. However, don't use past incidents to justify labeling specific students as troublemakers. Instead, help students who have experienced angry outbursts in the past feel welcome and valued in class by giving them a bit of extra attention. Planning for positive interactions on a systematic basis can be extremely effective in reducing the possibility or frequency of future incidents. |
| **2. Recognize That the Student Is Out of Control.** | Whenever possible, teachers should know their students well enough to be able to tell when a student has reached his or her breaking point. For some students, this might manifest as yelling or wild gestures. Others, however, might become very quiet or draw inward before erupting. It is particularly important to be aware of incidents that have the potential to provoke students, such as a recent fight or argument with another teacher or student. |
| **3. Put Physical Distance Between Yourself and the Student, and Avoid Threatening Behavior.** | When a student is extremely agitated and might act out physically, give the student enough physical space so that he or she doesn't feel threatened or provoked. Avoid using gestures or mannerisms that might be interpreted as aggressive, such as pointing your finger, raising your voice, squinting your eyes, furrowing your brows, moving toward the student, standing too close to the student, or hovering over the student. Rather, speak directly to the student in a calm and respectful voice. Look directly at the student without staring and keep your expressions as neutral as possible. Try to put distance between the student and other students in the class, especially if the student is lashing out at a peer. You might accomplish this by placing yourself between the aggressive student and the rest of the class or by asking the class to move to a specific location, such as one corner of the classroom. |

| | |
|---|---|
| **4. Calm Yourself.** | When a student lashes out or acts aggressively, it is natural to feel as if the student's outburst is a personal attack. To counteract these feelings and allow yourself to interact with the student in a calm and positive way, repeat positive affirmations to yourself, such as "This is not a personal attack on me; this student must be experiencing a great deal of pain and hurt to act in this way" or "This is just one moment in time. Help it to pass quickly without letting it harm anyone, including the student. Don't make things worse." |
| **5. Listen Attentively.** | Listen attentively to the student without agreeing or disagreeing with what he or she is saying. Use active listening skills, such as making eye contact and paraphrasing, to let the student know he or she is being heard. Keep your posture, expression, gestures, and tone of voice as neutral as possible as you focus on what the student is saying. When the student finishes speaking, respond with phrases such as "I think I understand how you feel" or "I understand what you're thinking." Then ask, "What else is bothering you?" Repeat this process until the student isn't able to think of anything else to say. At this point, the student will also likely be calmer due to feeling heard and understood. |
| **6. Remove the Student From the Situation.** | Once the student is calmer, use a simple, repeated request designed to remove the student from the situation (for example, "Billy, I'd like you to go with me out to the hallway to get things back to normal. Will you please do that with me now?"). Repeat your request calmly but persistently until the student complies. |
| **7. Set Up a Plan to Avoid Future Outbursts.** | About a day or so after the incident, connect with the student and communicate that you wish to re-establish the relationship and do not bear a grudge against the student for what happened. Talk about the incident, including why it occurred, and let the student know you hear and understand his or her thoughts and feelings. Create an action plan for future situations to ensure that the student will communicate with you before things escalate out of control. |

*Source: Adapted from Marzano, 2013.*

The process described in table 3.1 is designed to defuse a volatile situation and remove the agitated student from the situation as quickly as possible. This provides a safer environment for the offending student, the teacher, and the rest of the class.

# Being Sensitive to the Inner Worlds of Students

Maybe one of the most powerful outcomes of examining our own inner worlds and their effects on our lives is to realize that everyone with whom we come in contact has his or her own inner world and is constantly engaged in the same process as we are. They possess a hierarchy of goals and desired states. They continually interpret people, events, and tasks as situations that help them accomplish their goals and desired states or as obstacles to their goals and desired states. Some situations they encounter provoke reactions of fear and anger, which elicit a fight-or-flight response.

Knowing this might help us think differently about troublesome students. When we perceive a student to be misbehaving or acting disrespectfully, we might remember that these actions are nothing more than a script the student is executing based on some perceived threat to one of his or her goals or desired states. This is not to say that we should ignore misbehavior or disrespect. It is to say that we should always be sensitive to the fact that students are acting in accord with their beliefs about how the world works and are almost always trying to protect themselves in some way.

Sometimes it helps to know just how difficult the lives of some of our students can be. In her practice, Jana has worked with numerous students from primary school through high school. The following two stories illustrate the harsh circumstances students might experience in their home environments. Fair warning: these stories are not easy to read, but they are true and represent the day-to-day reality of some of the students you might encounter.

*Betsy was the fifth daughter in a row to her parents, but they desperately wanted a boy to carry on the family name. Her mother went into a depression because she felt the string of daughters was her fault and feared even more rages from her husband. Betsy was ignored and left to the care of her older sisters. While visiting her aunt and uncle without any of her sisters, she accidently walked in on her uncle raping her aunt. Shocked, she rushed to protect her aunt and was then assaulted herself. After that, Betsy withdrew into herself and did not speak much. As time went on, her parents had two sons and Betsy was truly left alone by her parents. With seven children, her mother needed to get a job, and Betsy was left in the care of her sisters for much of the day. Neighborhood boys sensed her vulnerability and began molesting her. Even so, during this time she was a cooperative, quiet, almost-straight-A student, mostly out of fear of her father's rages. But something was obviously amiss. Teachers noticed her staring into space, not paying attention, and having difficulty doing any type of group work. If a teacher reached out to help her, she would be too fearful of connection and say everything was fine and she was okay, when she was anything but okay.*

*Zach's mother was divorced twice from two men who didn't help with the bills or interact often with Zach. She ended up on government assistance and eked out a small living for the two of them. Out of her loneliness and fear, Zach's mother began using alcohol and drugs. Zach was left to fend for himself, eating whatever he could find, dressing poorly, and having poor hygiene. He was teased in school for his odd behavior and appearance and eventually began to fight back. He was constantly in trouble at school, but the usual disciplinary actions had no effect other than to make him feel even more isolated and misunderstood. While in middle school, running away, drinking, and taking drugs became his standard modes of operation. His teachers had no idea how to help him and generally left him alone.*

Given their home lives, it would be no wonder why Betsy or Zach might not be very attentive at school. Consequently, when we are interacting with students in any capacity, it is useful to remember that they might have lives like Betsy or Zach. Their actions, although interpreted negatively by us, might have little or nothing to do with us but are their mechanisms for survival in a very hostile world.

## Implications for Teaching

This chapter addressed the fact that managing the inner world is a skill that can be learned. Teachers should study and practice the steps of the process. Practice can and should occur retrospectively by considering people, events, and tasks that typically elicit strong negative reactions. It is advisable to start each day with a quick self-audit regarding the people, events, and tasks we will encounter. Those that might trigger unproductive scripts on our part should be prepared for so that they turn out as positively as possible. Truly dangerous situations should be defused as quickly and safely as possible. Finally, it is always useful to remember that the students and adults we encounter are also struggling with their own battles of negative interpretations and strong emotions and should be afforded some sympathy in our interactions with them. In the next chapter, we delve deeper into the workings of the human mind to help teachers understand why the management process is effective.

# Chapter 4

## *Delving Deep*

In some ways, managing the inner world opens Pandora's box as we become more and more curious about how the human mind works. In chapter 2, we addressed four topics that provided a grounding in the rudiments of the inner world. Those topics were (1) the power of emotions, (2) the nature of interpretation, (3) scripts, and (4) the importance of the self-system. This chapter addresses three other topics that provide a deeper understanding of the workings of the human mind: (1) mindfulness, (2) negative thinking, and (3) positive thinking.

## Mindfulness

In simple terms, mindfulness is being aware of what we are thinking about at a given moment. We might say that mindfulness is a precondition for managing the inner world. By definition, mindfulness involves a heightened state of consciousness. Understanding consciousness starts by understanding how three types of memory interact.

### Three Types of Memory

Recall from figure 1.1 (page 6) in chapter 1 that the inner world can be described in terms of the information that is occupying a teacher's working memory at any point in time. It is best to think of our working memory as one of three types of memory that interact with one another: (1) sensory memory, (2) working memory, and (3) permanent memory. The interaction of these three kinds of memory with the outside world is depicted in figure 4.1.

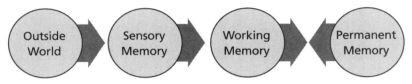

Source: Marzano & Pickering, 2011, p. 7.

**Figure 4.1: Interaction between three types of memory.**

Sensory memory addresses temporary storage of information from the senses. As indicated in figure 4.1, it is our conduit to the outside world. At any point in time, our sensory memory is storing sensory data coming in to us from our environment, such as smells, sights, sounds, and so on. John R. Anderson (1995) explained that sensory memory is capable of storing the majority of the sensory information encountered in brief intervals of time. However, if that information is not quickly encoded and utilized in working memory, then it is lost: "The environment typically offers much more information at one time than we can attend to and encode. Therefore much of what enters our sensory system results in no permanent record" (p. 160).

Working memory is where information is actively processed—hence the name *working* memory. As illustrated in figure 4.1, working memory can receive information from our external environment through sensory memory, or it can receive information from our permanent memory. Even though working memory can hold only small amounts of information, there is no theoretical limit to the amount of time information can reside in working memory. Once we are focusing on something, we can maintain that focus for long periods of time.

Permanent memory contains everything we have learned and all experiences we can remember. For example, our knowledge of the multiplication table is stored in permanent memory, as is our knowledge of the geographic makeup of the United States. Also, our permanent memory contains data representing what we did yesterday, at our last birthday, and other significant events in our lives. How we store our experiences in permanent memory provides even deeper insight into the inner world.

According to the dual coding theory as articulated by Allan Paivio (1969, 1971), information in permanent memory is encoded in two primary forms: (1) imagery and (2) language. Imagery information is expressed as mental pictures, kinesthetic associations, and sensory associations. For example, if we are recalling a pleasant event about a picnic from permanent memory and processing it in working memory, we will pull a mental picture or pictures about the event into our working memory. We also might re-experience the sounds, smells, and tastes that came through our sensory memory, the way our body felt, and even some of our emotions at that time.

Along with the imagery about the picnic, working memory will also pull up linguistic information from that pleasant event. The linguistic representation is commonly expressed as an inner dialogue (for example, Vygotsky, 1962) that includes our interpretation of the event—whether it was important or not, how it related to one or more of our goals and desired states, and so on. Some theorists have elevated language to a control position when used to interpret experiences. Indeed, philosopher Martin Heidegger (1977) referred to language as "the house of Being" (p. 217).

Permanent memory, then, is a rich source of experiences that can occupy our working memory at any point in time. These retrieved experiences come into our consciousness with a full complement of accessories—mental pictures, smells, sounds, emotions, and even a narrative that contains our judgment about the event we are recalling.

The three types of memory provide us with a better understanding of mindfulness. By definition, being mindful means being aware of what is currently in our working memory at any point in time. The information residing there might come from the outside world of the current situation in which we find ourselves, or it might come from the inside world of our permanent memory. In both cases, our working memory will contain images and language, the latter of which provides an accounting of how we are interpreting the situation.

## The Debate About Consciousness

While we are equating consciousness with what occupies our working memory, we should note that the topic of consciousness is one of the most discussed and debated in psychology and philosophy. While consciousness is certainly tied to the happenings within working memory, the historical discussions of human consciousness have gone well beyond consideration of what we are thinking about at any moment in time. For example, René Descartes's famous quote, "I think, therefore, I am" comes from his analysis of the very nature of consciousness, "Discourse on the Method of Rightly Conducting the Reason and Seeking Truth in the Sciences" (Descartes, 1637/1911, p. 101). For Descartes, the very fact that we can be conscious of our own thought processes was evidence of our existence as individual beings. In his book *Consciousness Explained*, Daniel C. Dennett (1991) wrote that the concept of consciousness was initially considered so esoteric and mysterious that it was explained as separate from the functioning of the human brain. He noted that it was considered quite natural to think of

> the self and its brain . . . as two distinct things, with different properties, no matter how closely they depend on each other. If the self is distinct from the brain, it seems that it must be made of mind stuff. In Latin, a thinking thing is a *res cogitans*, a term made famous by Descartes, who offered what he thought was an unshakable proof that he, manifestly a thinking thing, could not be his brain. (p. 29)

The idea that consciousness is not limited to working memory became known as dualism. Dennett (1991) explained, "The idea of mind as distinct in this way from the brain, composed not of ordinary matter but of some other, special kind of stuff, is *dualism*"

(p. 33). The discussion about the exact nature of consciousness is still in full force (see for example, *The Conscious Mind* [Chalmers, 1996] or *Irreducible Mind* [Kelly et al., 2007]). While the debate about dualism is interesting, any position one takes on it is compatible with the model we have provided about the inner world. However, we introduce the discussion to underscore the fact that the human mind is a very complex mechanism. Attempts like ours to describe its basic mechanisms are certainly useful but most probably only scratch the surface in terms of the intricacies of human behavior.

## Mental Control

Mental control is quite obviously related to mindfulness, which is quite obviously related to managing the inner world. Daniel M. Wegner and James W. Pennebaker (1993) explained that at its simplest level, mental control is a function of attention and focus—being aware of our thinking at any point in time and exerting control of our thoughts so as to enhance our current mental state or improve our performance on some task at hand. Not surprisingly, this is a good operational definition of managing the inner world. Thus, the concept of managing the inner world has been around for quite some time if we consider mindfulness and mental control as its predecessors.

Wegner and Pennebaker (1993) explained that William James was the most noteworthy early proponent of the concept of mental control. In 1890, James

> saw mental control as an effort akin to physical effort, and he wrote convincingly that moving the mind is like moving the muscles. And just as the muscles might operate on reflex, James held that attention could be wrested in various directions involuntarily as well. (Wegner & Pennebaker, 1993, p. 4)

More recently, Wegner and Pennebaker (1993) described mental control in the following way:

> If the simple mechanism of a thermostat can regulate the temperature in a room, it makes sense that the complex mechanism of a person can regulate much more, including even the person's own mental states or processes. The idea that control is executed by some "higher order" mechanism upon various "lower order" mechanisms is often important to this logic. A self-regulation approach to mental control takes this observation as the first step and goes on to propose how control mechanisms might be arranged to produce the wide array of mental states observed in human psychology. (p. 5)

It is interesting that Wegner and Pennebaker evoked the analogy of a thermostat when describing mental control. This, of course, evokes the image of the mind as a cybernetic mechanism. But Wegner and Pennebaker warned that mental control is not easy: "In an era of self-improvement and health consciousness, we have been struck by how often people attempt and fail to control themselves" (p. 2). Daniel M. Wegner and Ralph Erber (1993) echoed these same thoughts:

> Mental control may be a valued ideal, but it is seldom achieved or perfected to the degree that it characterizes broad stretches of our lives. It is perhaps far more typical for individuals to be filled with worries and second thoughts in interaction, trying not to let their private thoughts or emotions leak through. (p. 51)

In effect, mental control (also known as *mindfulness* or *managing the inner world*) requires a dedication to developing a level of self-discipline not easily attained, especially when we consider the natural tendency of the mind to wander.

## Mind Wandering

Apparently, the human mind has a natural tendency to wander. Michael D. Mrazek, Jonathan Smallwood, and Jonathan W. Schooler (2012) noted that "in direct contrast to mindfulness, which entails a capacity to avoid distraction, mind-wandering is characteristically described as the interruption of task focus by task-unrelated thought" (p. 442). Mind wandering constitutes as much as 50 percent of our waking thoughts (Killingsworth & Gilbert, 2010). Smallwood and Schooler (2013) explained that when the mind wanders, attention may become divided between internal and external information, a phenomenon described as "decoupling" (p. 138). They noted, "mind wandering can be viewed as a state of decoupled attention, because instead of monitoring online sensory information, attention shifts inward and focuses on one's thoughts and feelings" (p. 138).

The diagram in figure 4.1 (page 48) depicting the relationships among the various types of memory sheds light on Smallwood and Schooler's (2013) comments. What Smallwood and Schooler referred to as "online sensory information" is the information coming from the outside world; one's "thoughts and feelings" are the experiences stored in permanent memory. Mind wandering ignores the outside world, because we are focused solely on the inner world of our permanent memory. It is important to note that mind wandering is not necessarily a negative phenomenon. Bernard J. Baars (2010) noted:

> The stream of spontaneous thought is remarkably rich and self-relevant, reflecting one's greatest personal concerns, interpersonal feelings, unfulfilled goals and unresolved challenges, worries and hopes, inner debates, self-monitoring, feelings of knowing, visual imagery, imaginary social interactions, recurrent beliefs, coping reactions, intrusive memories, daydreams and fantasies, future plans, and more—all of which are known to guide the stream of thought. (p. 208)

There are times when it is useful to be lost in our thoughts, cut off from the outside world. Indeed, this occurs when we read something of interest. Smallwood (2013) explained, "It is also known, however, that the capacity to become immersed in the story that one is reading entails activation of many of the same neural processes that are engaged during mind wandering" (p. 529). It is also an aspect of a phenomenon known as incubation (Baird et al., 2012). Incubation occurs when we think deeply about a problem or task for an extended period of time. If our thinking is deep and focused enough, it benefits us even when we move our attention away from the problem or task. This explains, in part, why it sometimes appears that answers "pop" into our minds after we have been thinking about a problem or task. The rich stream of thought has produced something of use to us that finally becomes apparent.

Mindfulness, mental control, and managing the inner world, then, are not states we should seek to achieve on a permanent basis. Rather, we should seek a healthy balance. George A. Bonanno and Jerome L. Singer (1993) concluded that our thinking is most effective when we learn how to effectively shift attention between the inner and outer worlds:

> We propose that humans constantly must adapt to shifting their attention between the external environment and an ongoing thought stream. In ongoing thought we first assimilate this new external information into established memory schemas, assign meanings . . . and then next become aware of memories or fantasies, possible future events or possible selves . . . which we must somehow control and direct. This control may take a variety of forms. It can occur through shutting off attention to the stimuli generated from long-term memory almost entirely by a kind of flight into processing external stimulation . . . or by selective processing of only positive memories. (p. 150)

The ability to successfully switch between internal and external processes can be cultivated through mindfulness training.

## Mindfulness Training

One of the more promising aspects of mindfulness is that it can be developed with training and practice. Robert W. Roeser and his colleagues (2013) conducted a study of the effects of mindfulness training with teachers. They explained:

> Through mindfulness training . . . individuals are taught how to monitor their internal reactions to emotionally evocative situations and thereby know when they are in the grips of an emotion and need to take time to calm down before responding. In addition, individuals who undertake

> MT [mindfulness training] are taught how to cultivate an attitude of kindness and compassion toward themselves, especially during moments of difficulty that inevitably arise on the job and in life more generally. (p. 787)

During an eight-week program that involved eleven short sessions after school, elementary and secondary teachers were involved in a mindfulness training program. As described by Roeser and his colleagues (2013), the findings suggested that

> mindfulness training holds promise for the improvement of teaching and learning in public schools by assisting teachers in managing job stress and feelings of burnout more effectively. . . . By helping teachers to develop self-regulatory resources to meet the cognitive, social, and emotional demands of teaching, mindfulness training also may help teachers to conserve precious motivational and self-regulatory resources for investment in relationships with students and classroom teaching rather than coping and defense. (p. 802)

Managing the inner world, then, can be the subject of successful professional development. A central premise of this book is that managing the inner world is attainable by all teachers with the proper understanding of the human mind and the requisite practice.

# Negative Thinking

In chapter 2, we saw that strong negative emotions like fear and anger can have deleterious effects on our thinking and our actions. Here we consider broader patterns of negative thinking and their effects. Specifically, we consider habitual patterns of negative thought, worry, rumination, and primary negative events.

## Habitual Patterns of Negative Thought

There are some classic habitual patterns of negative thinking that have been described by various researchers and theorists. Combining the work of Matthew McKay, Martha Davis, and Patrick Fanning (2011) and Dennis C. Turk and Frits Winter (2006), we present the patterns of negative thought identified in table 4.1. We should note that these categories are certainly overlapping and are quite varied in terms of their influence on our thoughts and actions.

The list in table 4.1 is daunting, particularly when we recognize that we sometimes engage in one or more of these negative types of thinking. Such an awareness should not be cause for alarm. All of us occasionally engage in one or more of these types of thinking but we must take note of any negative pattern we engage in regularly or habitually. For example, assume we notice that we frequently engage in the mind-reading pattern of thought. While interacting with others, we make assumptions about what they are thinking and then act on these assumptions. If we assume someone is thinking negatively about us, we react in kind. Simply being aware of such a tendency can help us identify and guard against the unintended consequences of negative reactions on our part.

Another reason we should be aware of habitual patterns of negative thinking is that they are a source of constant agitation. Recall the discussion in chapter 2 about how our hectic environment can prime us to activate catecholamines, the chemicals that cue the fight-or-flight response. In effect, habitual negative patterns of thinking keep us close to the threshold of strong negative emotions. This is not a good situation for a harried teacher who faces a day filled with difficult situations.

## Worry

Worry is one of the most common forms of negative thinking. When left unchecked, it can take up a great deal of available space and time in working memory. It has been defined or described in many ways. Kevin D. McCaul and Amy B. Mullens (2003) explained that "worry has been conventionally defined as a chain of thoughts and images, which are negatively affect-laden and relatively uncontrollable" (p. 143). Andrew Mathews (1990) defined worry as "the persistent awareness of possible future danger, which is repeatedly rehearsed without being resolved" (p. 456).

## Table 4.1: Common Thinking Errors and Patterns of Negative Thinking

| Error | Description |
|---|---|
| Blaming | Blaming occurs when people start holding others responsible for the negative situations they are in or when they blame themselves for things that are out of their control. |
| "Should" Statements | When someone uses a "should" statement, he or she is subtly dictating rules about how others should act. This causes anger toward people who do not meet expectations or guilt when the person using the "should" statements violates his or her self-imposed rules. |
| Polarized Thinking | Polarized thinking distorts a person's vision of reality by eliminating the middle ground. Rather, people who use polarized thinking exclusively see failure or success or good or bad, without ever seeing improvement or progress. |
| Catastrophizing | Catastrophizing is a common thinking error in which people always expect the worst possible outcome. People who catastrophize often use "what if" statements to verbalize their negative imaginations. |
| Control Fallacies | There are two types of control fallacies: external and internal. The fallacy of external control causes people to feel helpless and see themselves as victims of others or of fate. On the other hand, the fallacy of internal control causes people to feel responsible for the well-being of all the people around them. |
| Emotional Reasoning | Emotional reasoning is when someone assumes that what he or she feels emotionally is what is true in reality. For example, if a person *feels* useless, he or she must *be* useless. |

Continued →

| Error | Description |
|---|---|
| Filtering | When people filter, they are unable or unwilling to see the positive aspects of their lives and constantly amplify the negative aspects of their lives. |
| Entitlement Fallacy | The entitlement fallacy is when people feel that they shouldn't have to experience discomfort that is a normal part of life (illness, aging, death, loss, and so on). These people feel entitled to escape these normal parts of life and find it unfair when they do experience them. |
| Fallacy of Fairness | The fallacy of fairness is a common thinking error in which an individual gets upset because he or she "knows" what is fair, yet other people don't necessarily agree with him or her. |
| Mind Reading | When people use mind reading in their everyday lives, they make and act upon assumptions about what the people around them are thinking or feeling. Normally, they do this without ever getting confirmation about these feelings from others. |
| Overgeneralizing | Someone who overgeneralizes concludes that a single situation or event is characteristic of all other events. These overgeneralizations are often inherently negative, so if something goes wrong once, it will go wrong over and over again. |
| Personalization | Personalization is when a person believes that everything others do or say is a direct reaction to him or her. These people also regularly compare themselves to others as a way to figure out who's smarter, more handsome, funnier, and so on, and then use these measures as a way to judge themselves. |

| Error | Description |
|---|---|
| **Fallacy of Change** | In the fallacy of change, a person depends on others changing in order to be happy. This person ultimately ends up pressuring others to do what he or she wants because he or she expects that others will change themselves to ensure his or her happiness. |
| **Global Labeling** | Global labeling is the practice of generalizing one or two negative qualities into all-encompassing judgments about oneself or others. |
| **Being Right** | People who fall victim to being right must be correct all the time with their words or actions. These people have to continually prove their "rightness," as if they're constantly being put on trial. |
| **Heaven's Reward Fallacy** | This fallacy is a common thinking error in which people sacrifice for others and secretly keep score. People who do this expect that down the road, their "debts" will be paid off. When the reward doesn't come, these people feel embittered at individuals, the world, or themselves. |

*Source: Adapted from McKay et al., 2011 and Turk & Winter, 2006.*

Worry is a phenomenon that begins quite early in life. To illustrate, in 2007, a survey by Nemours Foundation/KidsHealth, Department of Health Education and Recreation, and the National Association of Health Education Centers asked 1,154 children aged nine to thirteen how much they worried about a variety of concerns that are typical in that age interval. The majority of children (86 percent) said they worry "almost all of the time" or "a lot" about the health of someone they love. Many children said they worry "almost all the time" or "a lot" about other things, including schoolwork, tests, or grades (77 percent), their future (76 percent), and looks or appearance (63 percent). Table 4.2 (page 60) summarizes the results from that study.

**Table 4.2: KidsHealth Survey Results for Worry**

| Reason for Worry | Percentage of Kids Who Worry "Almost All of the Time" | Percentage of Kids Who Worry "A Lot" |
|---|---|---|
| Health of Loved One | 55 | 31 |
| The Future | 43 | 33 |
| Schoolwork, Tests, or Grades | 37 | 40 |
| Looks or Appearance | 37 | 26 |
| Making Mistakes or Messing Up | 26 | 35 |
| Friends and Their Problems | 24 | 33 |
| War or Terrorism | 25 | 25 |
| The Environment | 10 | 21 |

*Source: Adapted from Nemours Foundation/KidsHealth et al., 2007.*

Older people are also afflicted with worry, although at lower levels than young people. A study by Christine E. Gould and Barry A. Edelstein (2010) found that while older adults worry less often than young adults and have higher levels of control over their worry than their younger counterparts, they still experience anxiety, particularly over health-related concerns. In effect, worry is with us most of our lives.

Lizabeth Roemer and Thomas D. Borkovec (1993) provided the following humorous but accurate accounting of a typical episode of worry:

> Oh, no! The muffler sounds bad. . . . What if I have to take it to the shop? . . . I don't have time right now. . . . Business report is due in one week! . . . I can't afford the expense. . . . I'd have to draw the money from Jamie's college fund. . . . What if I can't afford his tuition? . . . I can't disappoint him, and it's so important that he get his degree. . . . That bad school report last week. . . . What if his grades go down and he can't get into college? . . . He and Martha aren't getting along. . . . I wish they'd be less angry with each other. . . . She hasn't seemed very affectionate to me, lately, either. . . . Maybe I could take her out to dinner this week. . . . No time, report due, how am I going to finish it? . . . Boss'll freak out. . . . Muffler sounds bad. . . . (p. 220)

Although written from a tongue-in-cheek perspective, Roemer and Borkovec's account of worry makes salient some interesting aspects of an episode of worry. It starts with a specific concern—in the example, the muffler sounds bad. It quickly moves to an outcome that will likely occur as a result of the initial concern—taking the car to the shop. That imagined action is then associated with one or more problem situations—"I can't afford it." These problem situations are associated with imagined actions that have their own negative consequences—"I will have to draw the money out of Jamie's account," and so on. Such thinking might lead the worrier anywhere, including back to the original concern—the muffler sounds bad.

Worry is commonly experienced as inner dialogue. As we have discussed, our thoughts are stored and experienced in two ways— images and language. Worry commonly manifests linguistically. As noted before, we narrate and editorialize our thoughts. Roemer and Borkovec (1993) explained:

> People report that their worry mostly involves talking to themselves, largely about problems or negative events that have happened or might happen in the future and mental

attempts to figure out how to solve those problems or avoid those events, with brief catastrophic images of the negative events symbolized by the words flowing through their minds. The content of the worrying frequently jumps from one concern to another concern, with elements of the entire episode repeating themselves. Brief problem-solving attempts rarely reach a resolution for any single element. (p. 220)

At its best, worry occupies our consciousness with thoughts that are not productive. As mentioned by Roemer and Borkovec, attempts to solve the problems, real or imagined, during episodes of worry are rarely effective. Worry can also have more severe consequences. For example, Rebecca J. Compton and David A. Mintzer (2001) found that high levels of worry inhibit communication between the left and right hemispheres of the brain. In its extreme form, worry can devolve into rumination.

## Rumination

Rumination is one of the most severe types of negative thinking. It is "generally defined as repetitive thinking about negative personal concerns and/or about the implications, causes, and meanings of a negative mood" (Whitmer & Gotlib, 2013, p. 1036). In their review of the research on rumination, Anson J. Whitmer and Ian H. Gotlib (2013) found that it appears to influence the efficiency and manner in which we process information in working memory. Table 4.3 summarizes some of the findings they reported.

Once a tendency to worry reaches the level of rumination, it has changed our life for the worse. Episodes of worry are replaced by obsessive thinking about situations and problems that cannot be solved by continual examination. In effect, rumination takes us away from experiencing life. We fill our working memory with concerns spawned from the inner world of our permanent memory. Little time is left to experience the outside world through our senses.

## Table 4.3: Summary of Research on Possible Effects of Rumination

| Study | Conclusions About Rumination |
|---|---|
| **Berman et al., 2011** | Related to difficulties switching between two goals |
| **Compton, Fisher, Koenig, McKeown, & Muñoz, 2003** | Related to bias toward accessing perceptual information in the right hemisphere of the brain as opposed to semantic information in the left |
| **Davis & Nolen-Hoeksema, 2000** | Related to greater perseveration |
| **Hertel, 1998** | Related to impairment in the control of memory retrieval |
| **Joormann, 2006** | Related to less inhibition of irrelevant emotions |
| **Joormann & Gotlib, 2008** | Related to decreased ability to inhibit no-longer-relevant negative, but not positive, information held in working memory |
| **Joormann, Levens, & Gotlib, 2011** | Related to difficulties reversing the order of negative, but not positive, information held in working memory |
| **Joorman & Tran, 2009** | Related to decreased inhibition of previously relevant negative information (but not positive information) |
| **Watkins & Brown, 2002** | Inhibited ability to generate random numbers |
| **Whitmer & Banich, 2011** | Inhibited performance in laboratory-controlled learning tasks |
| **Whitmer, Frank, & Gotlib, 2012** | Inhibited performance in laboratory-controlled learning tasks |

*Source: Whitmer & Gotlib, 2013.*

Left unchecked, rumination can lead to depression. Edward R. Watkins and Susan Nolen-Hoeksema (2014) explained that "depressive rumination is the tendency to repetitively analyze oneself and one's problems, concerns, and feelings of distress and depressed mood" (p. 24). At a general level, they described rumination in the following way:

> During rumination, negative thought content, negative context (e.g., negative mood), and abstract-evaluative thinking focused on the meaning and implications of negative events (e.g., asking "Why?") relative to concrete thinking, focused on the details, process, and context of negative events (e.g., asking "How?"), contribute to unconstructive outcomes. (p. 24)

Of course, depression is a vast topic in its own right and is far beyond the scope of this book. Briefly though, depression is an illness that many people suffer from at some point in their lives. The *Diagnostic and Statistical Manual of Mental Disorders* (American Psychiatric Association, 2013) stated that about 2–9 percent of the U.S. adult population is clinically depressed at any one time, with a lifetime risk of 10–25 percent of women and 5–12 percent of men. The symptoms include at least two weeks of lost interest in pleasurable activities, moods of sadness and/or irritability, and often, changes in sleeping, eating, and energy levels. When we are depressed, we can experience feelings of guilt, worthlessness, and even thoughts of suicide and death. There is also occupational, cognitive, and social impairment. We may notice that common tasks are harder, such as parenting and exercise, and we may be more prone to alcohol and drug abuse.

There are a variety of effective treatments for depression which can be accessed at doctors' offices, community mental health centers, and with private practitioners. Many updated drugs are available, as are behavioral treatment methods that are not always expensive. Untreated depression is debilitating, with conditions ranging from increased risk of dementia to a heightened risk for falls, bone fractures, diabetes, and death from other diseases (Remedy Health Media, 2015). For these reasons, we recommend prompt treatment using the many resources available to all.

## Primary Negative Events

Strong negative reactions to situations can be due to primary negative events that might have occurred in our lives. A primary negative event is an incident that results in substantial physical and/ or psychological harm to an individual. Typically, these events occur relatively early in life and are situations over which we had little or no control. In the extreme, primary negative events can cause an individual to suffer from post-traumatic stress disorder (PTSD; Shapiro, 1996). For example, an individual who has experienced the primary negative event of observing family members being killed might re-experience that event any time something happens that is even remotely similar to the situation in which the traumatic event occurred.

The power of a primary negative event in terms of influencing our thinking stems from the fact that we tend to make linkages between past events and current events quite quickly and automatically. This is due to a phenomenon known as "spreading activation." In a series of works, Anderson (1983, 1990a, 1990b, 1993, 1995) articulated the *theory of spreading activation*. Fundamentally, the theory postulates that any new situation we encounter, once classified, activates all similar past situations. For example, assume a teacher had experienced a primary negative event as a child in which she was beaten up by a girl who had a scar on the left side of her face. While this incident was not life threatening, it was traumatic in the sense that she was quite frightened while it was happening. As we have seen, since that event surely evoked the fight-or-flight response from her, it was stored in permanent memory in a way that it can be readily recalled. In addition to easily recalling the event, spreading activation theory dictates that any future events with similar characteristics could quickly connect the teacher back to this primary event. If the teacher encountered a person with a scar on the left side of his or her face, this similar characteristic would activate the primary negative event. While the teacher might not be aware that the event had been activated, she would be re-experiencing a fight-or-flight response. Again, this is not an ideal situation for a busy teacher who interacts with scores of students on a daily basis.

# Positive Thinking

If there are negative patterns of thought that can hamper our ability to manage the inner world, there are also positive patterns of thought that can enhance our managerial acumen. Positive thinking is a critical aspect of what is referred to as *resiliency*. In their book, *Resilience: The Science of Mastering Life's Greatest Challenges*, Southwick and Charney (2012) defined resilient people as those who "bounce back" (p. 1) after trying events occur in their lives. Not only do they make it through negative events with little apparent damage but they also use those experiences to gain new strength and develop new skills.

Norman Garmezy popularized the concept of resilience as it relates to education in 1974 in an article in a technical journal where he reported on children who had overcome the effects of potentially traumatizing negative events. Bonnie Benard (2004), Tan Phan (2003), Lillian B. Rubin (1996), and others have also added to an understanding of the concept of resiliency, particularly as it relates to education. One type of thinking associated with resiliency is optimism.

## Optimism

It is interesting and instructive to note that Southwick and Charney (2012) qualified the concept of optimism with the adjective *realistic*. They explained:

> Contrary to popular belief, resilient optimists rarely ignore the negative in life by viewing the world through "rose-

colored glasses." In their book *The Resilience Factor*, Karen Reivich and Andrew Shatté (2003) refer to this as "realistic optimism." Like pessimists, realistic optimists pay close attention to negative information that is relevant to the problems they face. However, unlike pessimists, they do not remain focused on the negative. They tend to disengage rapidly from problems that appear to be unsolvable. That is, they know when to cut their losses and turn their attention to problems that they believe they can solve. (p. 29)

An optimistic pattern of thinking, then, addresses both the negative and positive aspects of a situation. Diane L. Coutu (2002) noted that in challenging situations, "a cool, almost pessimistic, sense of reality is far more important. . . . Facing reality, really facing it, is grueling work. Indeed, it can be unpleasant and often emotionally wrenching" (p. 48).

Some of the earliest popular accounts of optimism are found in the writings of Norman Vincent Peale. In 1952, Peale published *The Power of Positive Thinking* which, according to Southwick and Charney (2012), has sold over five million copies since its publication. Southwick and Charney described Peale's recommendations in the following way:

- Make a true estimate of your ability and then raise it 10%.
- Formulate and stamp indelibly on your mind a mental picture of yourself as succeeding. Always picture success no matter how badly things seem to be going at the moment.
- Practice positive and peaceful thinking by making a list of positive and peaceful thoughts and pass them through your mind several times each day.
- Practice the technique of suggestive articulation, that is, repeat audibly some positive, success-oriented and peaceful words.
- Do not build up obstacles in your imagination.
- Adopt an "I don't believe in defeat" attitude.
- Start each day by affirming positive, successful, peaceful, and happy attitudes and your days will tend to be pleasant and successful. (p. 40)

Thirteen years after Peale's initial work, Martin E. P. Seligman took a more clinical and balanced approach to optimism, initially based on studies with animals. His now-famous study in 1965 focused on the phenomenon of *learned helplessness* in dogs. In his experiment, one group of dogs was exposed to a mild electric shock but had the opportunity to jump over a barrier to escape. A second group of dogs was exposed to mild shocks with no means of escape. The third group received no shocks. Following this first round of treatment, all the dogs were exposed to shocks that they could avoid by jumping the barrier. The first and third groups easily escaped, but the dogs from the second group—who had no way to avoid the shocks in the first round—just lay down and waited for the discomfort to end. They were conditioned to be helpless. The dogs' attitudes appeared to be rather flexible, though, as Seligman was able to retrain them to avoid the shock (Seligman, 2006).

As described in *Learned Optimism* (2006), Seligman later conducted a learned helplessness experiment with humans. In that variation, the three groups were exposed to unpleasant sounds rather than electric shocks. Again, the first group could turn off the sound, the second group could do nothing about it, and the third group did not experience the noise. In the second phase of the experiment, the people responded in a manner similar to the dogs': the first and third groups quickly figured out how to extinguish the noise, but most people in the second group had learned helplessness and made no effort. This result was not, however, as consistent as the result with the dogs—there were some people who did not learn helplessness, and some people who could not later *un*learn it. These people who displayed inherent tendencies led Seligman to conduct further research on people's general outlooks on life.

Seligman posited that the inherent optimism or helplessness that people in the experiment displayed was reflective of their *explanatory style*—how they explain positive and negative life events to themselves. For example, a person with a negative explanatory style might view negative life events as being his or her own fault and view positive life events as accidental or due to outside forces. Seligman and his colleagues explored this attribute and its effects on students over time. They studied four hundred third graders for five years and used observations of their life events and explanatory styles to make predictions about which students would exhibit depression and low academic performance in the future. A negative explanatory style was strongly associated with depression and poor performance, while a positive explanatory style helped students deal with tough times in their lives and succeed academically. Adults displayed similar consequences of explanatory styles. A long-term study of men beginning in the 1930s showed that a positive explanatory style and outlook in early adulthood led to increased health and happiness later in life (as cited in Seligman, 2006).

Based on this research, Seligman (2006) identified three aspects of explanatory styles: (1) permanence, (2) pervasiveness, and (3) personalization. Table 4.4 (page 70) describes how a person with an optimistic or pessimistic style would explain negative or positive life events in terms of each aspect.

*Permanence* refers to whether we view an event as short term or long term—that is, temporary or permanent. High permanence for negative events (that is, a pessimistic style) means that we view a negative event as the result of an ever-present aspect of our life (such as persistent bad luck), whereas if we have low permanence for negative events (that is, an optimistic style), we view the same event as a temporary misstep. High permanence for positive events, on the other hand, helps us view positive events as the result of long-term traits (such as our work ethic). In contrast, if we have low permanence for positive events, we tend to view good things as unusual incidents.

*Pervasiveness* refers to how much an isolated event is perceived to affect the rest of our life. If we have high pervasiveness for negative events, we let those events influence other parts of our lives (for example, becoming an overly cautious driver after getting injured in a volleyball game). If we have low pervasiveness for negative events,

**Table 4.4: Elements of Explanatory Styles**

| Aspect | Event Type | Optimistic | Pessimistic |
|---|---|---|---|
| **Permanence** | *Bad things* | **Temporary:** Temporary circumstances in my life cause the bad things that happen to me. | **Permanent:** Permanent elements of my life cause the bad things that happen to me. |
| | *Good things* | **Permanent:** Permanent elements of my life cause the good things that happen to me. | **Temporary:** Temporary circumstances in my life cause the good things that happen to me. |
| **Pervasiveness** | *Bad things* | **Specific:** When a bad thing happens in one area of my life, it doesn't negatively affect other parts of my life. | **Universal:** When a bad thing happens in one area of my life, it ruins my whole life. |
| | *Good things* | **Universal:** When a good thing happens in one area of my life, it makes my whole life better. | **Specific:** When a good thing happens in one area of my life, it doesn't positively affect other parts of my life. |
| **Personalization** | *Bad things* | **External:** A bad thing happened to me because of factors out of my control. | **Internal:** A bad thing happened to me because I didn't do something right. |
| | *Good things* | **Internal:** A good thing happened to me because I did something right. | **External:** A good thing happened to me because of factors out of my control. |

we are more likely to isolate the effects of a single event. In contrast, high pervasiveness for positive events allows us to spread the positive effects of an event (such as confidence from a successful date) to other parts of our life, while low pervasiveness for positive events prevents this.

*Personalization* refers to whether we view events as caused by internal (personal) or external factors. If we have high personalization for negative events, we blame ourselves when something goes wrong. If we have low personalization for negative events, we blame other factors or people. If we have high personalization for positive events, we take credit for good things that happen to us, while low personalization for positive events leads us to give credit to other people.

Seligman's model provides a quick reference for our tendencies toward optimism versus pessimism. Specifically, simply looking through the statements in table 4.4 and determining whether we are in the optimistic column versus the pessimistic column gives a good sense of our tendency toward a positive (that is, optimistic) explanatory style versus a negative (that is, pessimistic) explanatory style.

## Meaning and Purpose

Another powerful type of positive thinking involves seeking out and finding meaning and purpose in life. Southwick and Charney (2012) explained that having meaning and purpose in our lives allows us to view hardship from a unique perspective:

> When philosopher Frederick Nietchze [sic] wrote, "He who has a why can endure almost any how," he was referring to the power of meaning. Other renowned scholars have also recognized the powerful effects of meaning; of having a worthy goal or mission in life. As Carl Jung wrote in his classic book *Man and His Symbols*, "[Man] can stand the most incredible hardships when he is convinced they make sense" (1968, p. 76). South African dissident Nelson Mandela stands as an inspiring example: Mandela was able to tolerate 30 years of imprisonment with grace and dignity because his imprisonment symbolized the struggle for equality. Meaning can give us strength and meaning can

give us courage. During your own life, when called upon to defend a cherished idea, stand up for a worthy cause, or protect a loved one, perhaps you have been surprised by the reservoir of strength and resilience that lies within. (p. 184)

In his book *Man's Search for Meaning*, Viktor E. Frankl (1963) made the point that meaning is highly personal—what is meaningful to one person might not be meaningful to another person. However, everyone needs meaning in their lives, particularly during times of intense difficulty. Viktor Frankl's life itself is a testament to the power of meaning and purpose.

Frankl was born and raised in Vienna in the early 1900s. He was intensely interested in people and, as a result, pursued studies in psychology during the early years of his life. By 1938, when Hitler's troops invaded Austria, he had earned his medical degree and had opened his own private practice in neurology and psychiatry. Frankl married in 1942, but in September of that year, Frankl and his wife, father, mother, and brother were all arrested and taken to Theresienstadt, a concentration camp in Czechoslovakia (now the Czech Republic). His father died at Theresienstadt, his mother and brother were killed at Auschwitz in 1944, and his wife died at Bergen-Belsen in 1945. Frankl himself was moved to Auschwitz and then two other concentration camps. In 1945, Frankl's camp was liberated and he returned to Vienna, only to discover that all of his loved ones were dead (with the exception of his sister Stella, who had emigrated to Australia). Although he was crushed, Frankl continued his studies in psychology, focusing specifically on different people he had encountered in the concentration camps. Frankl realized that, in many cases, it was the people whose lives contained hope, meaning, and faith who were best able to survive the hardships and atrocities of the concentration camps and the Holocaust. In an article he wrote in 1958, Frankl said:

In my opinion man is dominated neither by the will-to-pleasure nor by the will-to-power, but what I call man's *will-to-meaning*, that is to say, his deep-seated striving and struggle for a higher and ultimate meaning to his existence. (p. 20)

While it is clear that meaning and purpose are important to a positive experience of life, it is not as clear how to access them. One fruitful avenue appears to be the process of inspiration.

## Inspiration

A significant amount of research and theory has been focused on the phenomenon of inspiration. Todd M. Thrash, Andrew J. Elliot, Laura A. Maruskin, and Scott E. Cassidy (2010) contended that inspiration is foundational to many processes we associate with meaning and purpose:

> Many of the experiences that individuals find most fulfilling —peak experiences . . . creative insights . . . spiritual epiphanies . . . and emotions of awe and elevation . . .—cannot be controlled or directly acquired, because they involve the transcendence of one's current desires, values, or expectations. Indeed, life would likely seem bland if one's strivings were never interrupted and informed by such experiences. We propose that *inspiration*, which is central to each of the above experiences, is an important influence on well-being. (p. 488)

Thrash and Elliot (2003) initially described inspiration as involving three core characteristics: (1) transcendence, (2) evocation, and (3) approach motivation. *Transcendence* refers to gaining an awareness of possibilities that are superior to our current circumstances. *Evocation* refers to the fact that inspiration is experienced as evoked; we don't feel like we are the cause of it. *Approach motivation* means that we feel compelled to do something as a result of our experience of inspiration. Later, Thrash and Elliott (2004) made a distinction between being inspired *by* and being inspired *to*. Being inspired *by* involves the appreciation of the vision generated by the inspiration. Being inspired *to* means being motivated to actualize the vision generated by the inspiration.

Darrell Scott and Robert J. Marzano (2014) provided a perspective on inspiration directly tied to the nature of the self-system. They explained that inspiration occurs when a person encounters evidence indicating that one of their fundamental beliefs about how the world works (or ought to work) is true. In chapter 2, we noted that the self-system involves a hierarchy of goals and desired states. Here we expand the concept of the self-system to include our beliefs about how the world works. In an early work, Frank Smith (1971/2004) referred to these beliefs as our "theory of the world":

> Everything that we know and believe is organized into a personal *theory* of what the world is like, a theory that is the basis of all our perceptions and understanding of the world, the root of all learning, the source of hopes and fears, motives and expectancies, reasoning and creativity. . . . If we can make sense of the world at all, it is by interpreting our experience with the world in the light of our theory. The theory is our shield against bewilderment. (p. 10)

Our theory of the world completes the picture of the self-system begun in chapter 2. We construct our theory of the world over time by creating generalizations and rules about what we believe the world to be and how we should behave in it to accomplish our goals and desired states. Recall from the discussion in chapter 2 that we are prone to categorize the world around us, and within each category, we develop rules and generalizations. We construct these categories for each of the six levels of goals and desired states. Stated differently, we have a theory of the world for each of the six levels of the hierarchy that constitute our self-system.

To illustrate, assume we have constructed rules and generalizations like the following for the six levels of our hierarchy.

Level 1  Warm places are comfortable to be in (physiology).

Level 2  Firearms are dangerous (safety).

Level 3  Friendly people tend to have friends (belonging within a community).

Level 4  People look up to you if you are an athlete (esteem within a community).

Level 5  Working outdoors makes people happy (self-actualization).

Level 6    If you work hard at something, people tend to rally around you and help you out (connection to something greater than self).

Each of these six rules and generalizations relates to a different level of the hierarchy of goals and desired states. The first generalization or rule deals with the need for physiological comfort. While the need itself is innate, the generalization that warm places are comfortable is part of our theory of the world that we construct over time. Once we have established the belief as part of our theory of the world, we seek out warm places to fulfill a physiological need. The second generalization relates to the need for safety, which is innate; the generalization that firearms are dangerous is part of our theory of the world. In short, for every level of the hierarchy, we build a theory about those things that will help us accomplish goals and desired states and those things that will not. These rules and generalizations tell us what situations should be considered negative and what situations should be considered positive because they will help or hinder our acquisition of a goal or desired outcome.

Up through the fifth level of the hierarchy (self-actualization), much of our constructed theory comes from our experiences. We observe that people look up to athletes and we construct a theory about how to establish a sense of esteem (level 4), we observe that people who work outdoors appear to be happy and we develop a theory about how to be self-actualized (level 5), and so on. However, at the sixth level of the hierarchy—connection to something greater than the self—concrete evidence is not easily observed. To illustrate, consider the rule for the sixth level stated previously. Most of us would like it to be true that if you work hard, people will rally around you and help you out. However, there are not a great many examples of this in day-to-day life. Rules and generalizations at the level of connection to something greater than the self are probably best described as *ideals*—those things about the world we would like to be true but are not completely sure actually are.

The ideals that constitute this sixth level explain inspiration. Namely, we are inspired when we observe, read about, or hear about events that provide evidence that one or more of our ideals are, in fact, true. For example, if we have the ideal that people rally around you if you work hard at something, then we will be inspired by the movie *Rudy*, in which the Notre Dame football team rallies around one of their players to help him realize a dream he has worked hard to achieve. If we have the ideal that humans and animals can have meaningful relationships, then we will be inspired by a story of a lost dog who travels hundreds of miles to find his master.

Inspiration, then, might be thought of as one of the highest forms of motivation, for it puts us in touch with those rules and generalizations from which we would like to operate—our ideals. If Viktor Frankl was correct about the fact that humankind is dominated by a search for meaning, then identifying and operating from our ideals should be a priority in our lives.

## Implications for Teaching

This chapter has delved deeply into the workings of the human mind, expanding on what was presented in chapter 2. This knowledge can enhance our ability to manage the inner world. The information about mindfulness provides a useful perspective on managing the inner world. Mindfulness involves being aware of what is in our working memory at any point in time. In effect, consciousness is defined by what is in working memory. It takes a great deal of mental energy and control to stay mindful of our thoughts because natural tendencies like mind wandering work against the discipline of mental control. While mental control should not be practiced all the time, it should be a skill that we can employ at will. This takes focus and practice.

The information about negative thinking adds to what was presented in chapter 2. There we found that strong emotions like anger and fear actually distort our thinking at specific moments in time, not allowing us to see alternatives we might consider if we were not angry or fearful. In this chapter, we expanded the discussion of specific negative emotions to include negative patterns of thinking and broad tendencies such as worry and rumination. Teachers should be aware of such tendencies and take proper precautions.

On the positive side of things, teachers can work to develop positive patterns of thinking. Optimism is a positive pattern of thinking that can be cultivated by examining one's explanatory style regarding beliefs about permanence, pervasiveness, and personalization when negative things occur in our lives. Another positive pattern of thinking is to seek meaning and purpose in our lives by identifying those ideals that provide a sense of connection to something greater than self—the highest level of the hierarchy of goals and desired states. In the next chapter, we turn our attention to a different arena in which teachers can profitably practice and apply the process for managing the inner world: their lives outside of school. We present specific ways to cultivate a healthier psychological lifestyle and avoid negative thinking patterns in a variety of situations.

# Chapter 5

*Working on Ourselves*

One obvious conclusion about managing the inner world of teaching is that it requires us to work on ourselves, especially when we consider how easy it is to be affected by the types of negative thinking described in chapter 4. By definition, examining our patterns of thought during specific incidents in school leads to examination of how we approach life in general. In this chapter, we address some ways we can cultivate a healthier psychological lifestyle. We address four topics: (1) performing a self-audit of our overall mental state, (2) using the management process in our daily lives, (3) cultivating satisfaction, and (4) identifying and living from our ideals.

## Performing a Self-Audit of Our Overall Mental State

To begin working on ourselves, it is useful to examine our overall mental health. We might think of such activity as a self-audit we use to diagnose areas in our life of strength and areas of concern. To this end, it is useful to consult figure 5.1 (page 80). It depicts a continuum of mental health with five levels moving from non-functional to superior functioning. The continuum is designed to provide a frame of reference as to our overall mental health. It is important to note that figure 5.1 should not be thought of as an absolute classification system. Rather, while examining ourselves in reference to the continuum, we will find that we operate at different

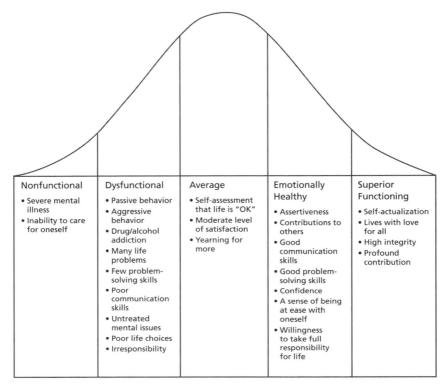

| Nonfunctional | Dysfunctional | Average | Emotionally Healthy | Superior Functioning |
|---|---|---|---|---|
| • Severe mental illness<br>• Inability to care for oneself | • Passive behavior<br>• Aggressive behavior<br>• Drug/alcohol addiction<br>• Many life problems<br>• Few problem-solving skills<br>• Poor communication skills<br>• Untreated mental issues<br>• Poor life choices<br>• Irresponsibility | • Self-assessment that life is "OK"<br>• Moderate level of satisfaction<br>• Yearning for more | • Assertiveness<br>• Contributions to others<br>• Good communication skills<br>• Good problem-solving skills<br>• Confidence<br>• A sense of being at ease with oneself<br>• Willingness to take full responsibility for life | • Self-actualization<br>• Lives with love for all<br>• High integrity<br>• Profound contribution |

*Source: Adapted from Marzano et al., 2005. Used with permission.*

**Figure 5.1: Mental health scale.**

levels in different aspects of our lives. As Marzano and his colleagues (2005) noted:

> It is important to realize that you probably exhibit behaviors from multiple categories. This is because throughout our lives, we are in one category at certain times but then move to another category later on. Additionally, we might exhibit the characteristics of different categories in different situations. You might notice, for example, that in school you have adopted many of the behaviors in the *emotionally healthy* category, but in some family situations you tend to adopt the behaviors in the *dysfunctional* category. Noticing this difference can lead to insights and, ultimately, to improvements in your viewpoint and actions. (pp. 95, 97)

At the lower end of the scale is the level *nonfunctional.* This level involves schizophrenia and major depression, tendencies that are well beyond what most of us ever have or will experience in our lives. Behaviors at this level should result in seeking immediate help from a trained professional (for example, a psychotherapist, psychologist, psychiatrist, pastor, rabbi, and so on). Unfortunately, individuals who find themselves at the nonfunctional level are just that; they can't function in the day-to-day world without the help of others to care for at least some of their daily needs. These needs might include medications, a safe and comfortable place to live, food, clothing, established routines, and so on. From the perspective of the hierarchy, these individuals most probably have experienced primary negative events in their lives relative to physiology, safety, and belonging.

The *dysfunctional* level is above the nonfunctional level. Although behavior at this level is well above that of the nonfunctional level, it still signals problems that must be dealt with. Some of these problems may stem from unresolved childhood issues, growing up in a dysfunctional household, or a lack of development of basic life skills. While individuals can operate in society at this level, they are severely hampered by these "ghosts from the past." These individuals might also have had issues in their past regarding basic needs for physiology, safety, or belonging.

The level above dysfunctional is *average.* At this level individuals feel okay about their lives, but there are still things missing. In terms of the hierarchy of goals and desired states, these individuals most probably have addressed their basic needs for physiology, safety, belonging, and even esteem within a community.

The level between average and superior functioning is *emotionally healthy.* These are people who consistently get along well with others, get things done, and make contributions to the lives of their family members and their coworkers. They are usually confident and self-assured. They create few problems and are able to resolve the problems they encounter effectively and efficiently. In terms of the hierarchy, they are at least self-actualized.

At the highest end of the continuum is the level *superior functioning*. This level of behavior represents life lived in a way that is self-actualizing and connected to causes greater than self. Certainly, individuals like Nelson Mandela, Mahatma Gandhi, and Mother Teresa operated in this manner. However, there are many individuals who have reached this level and not received public acclaim. As Marzano and colleagues (2005) noted, "This group also includes many 'ordinary' people who have mastered being human to the point where they can not only make contributions to their communities and families but also live their personal lives with love and integrity" (p. 95).

Figure 5.1 (page 80) should not be used as a global categorization of our lives. However, it is useful to consider our mental health in various aspects of our lives as a guide to what we might work on. To illustrate how this might manifest, consider the cases of Jerry and Lisa:

*Jerry decided to seek therapy to handle his difficulty starting his private practice in accounting. Upon analysis, he concluded that he was at the average level relative to his career. He was doing well, but there was something missing. He had successfully worked for other firms and felt somewhat confident he could make a go of it alone. However, he found himself making hiring mistakes and feeling depressed, defeated, and disorganized. As that was uncharacteristic of him in other aspects of his life, he was bewildered by his behavior, though it felt oddly familiar. On review of his background, he revealed that his father "drank a bit too much" and was a hoarder. The family had to move frequently because his father couldn't keep a job, "wasn't lucky," and had "no one to help him." His father believed that a rich uncle would realize his plight and help the family, though this never happened. On a deep level, Jerry also believed that he was incapable of making it on his own like his father and was indeed waiting to be rescued. Once this connection was made and resolved, Jerry was able to decide on a new, more adaptive belief for himself. He chose, "I have everything I need to be successful on my own." He has since been able to make better choices to get his business on track.*

---

*Lisa was a forty-year-old banker who was well-liked at her job. She had received many awards, and her career was accelerating. She met many interesting and successful men but sought therapy because she couldn't figure out why she ended up with dysfunctional partners even at this later stage of life. She concluded that she was functioning at least at the average level in her professional life, but was bordering on dysfunctional in terms of her relationships with men. Although she said her early life was fine in spite of her parents' divorce, a look at her background revealed information to the contrary. Lisa had a loving mother, whom she lived with after the divorce, but a father with Asperger's syndrome. He only felt comfortable working; socializing made him quite uncomfortable. From her observations of her father, Lisa learned that hard work is necessary but relationships aren't. This became part of her theory of the world. Because her father was, in her words, "strange and awkward," she tended to pick men who were charismatic and worldly but also had a variety of problems. However, Asperger's was not among the problems of any of her partners. This discrepancy made her miss the obvious connection to her father. Her belief system was, "Normal men will never want or stay with me." After working on this issue, she was able to pick a much healthier man as a partner.*

---

# Using the Management Process in Our Daily Lives

The core skill of managing the inner world is the three-phase process (awareness, analysis, and choice) introduced in chapter 1 and further exemplified for a teaching context in chapter 3. This management process can also be used in our lives outside of school. Here we consider its retrospective use as well as its real-time use.

## Retrospective Practice Outside of School

For retrospective practice, we might think of events, tasks, and people that typically elicit strong negative reactions in our daily lives. For example, consider a teacher who thinks about the events in his life outside of school and notices that he usually reacts negatively to driving to work. He begins by considering the awareness phase questions, What emotions do I experience? and What is my interpretation of this situation? In answer, he notices that driving in morning traffic makes him nervous and anxious and that he often interprets his morning drive as unfair since he and his wife live much closer to her workplace than to his school.

During the analysis phase, he considers the questions: What script do I typically execute as the result of my interpretation? What is the typical outcome of my actions? and Is the outcome something that is the most positive for all concerned? In response to his interpretation, he notes that he usually executes a script that involves leaving for work later than he should (because he doesn't look forward to the drive), driving to work as fast as possible without much consideration for other drivers, and talking to himself during the drive about how unhappy he is. The outcome of his actions is that he usually arrives at work disgruntled and angry. He recognizes that this outcome is not the most positive for all concerned, as he is normally grumpy toward his wife, late for work, angry every morning, and unpleasant to his coworkers and students once he gets to school.

Finally, for the choice phase, the questions are: What is my preferred outcome? and What script do I have to execute to attain this outcome? He concludes that a more preferred outcome would include leaving on time for work, feeling happy during his drive, and arriving at school in a positive frame of mind, ready to help his students and colleagues. To attain this outcome, he creates a new script for his morning drive. He adjusts his bedtime and waking time so that he has a few minutes to himself in the morning to get centered, calm, and ready for the day. He also establishes a routine that helps ensure he leaves for work on time. During his drive, he begins listening to classical music or books on tape, which calm him down and give him something to focus on other than traffic and the time. Once he gets to school, he takes three minutes before getting out of his car to calm down and says to himself, "I make a difference. Because of what I do, children have a greater chance of success in the world. I never know exactly what impact I'll have, so I'm going to make sure every interaction today is as positive as possible." Although it takes him a few weeks to get used to his new script and routine, he greatly prefers the new set of outcomes.

## Real-Time Practice Outside of School

The three phases and their related questions can also be used in real time as we encounter new situations throughout the day. To illustrate, assume that on a particular weekend, a teacher encounters the following situation: she and her husband are going out to dinner, and the host seats them at a table right by the kitchen door of the restaurant. It is noisy, and servers are constantly passing their table as they bring orders from the kitchen to the dining room. She immediately notices that her reaction is negative. She decides to use the management process. As a result of the awareness phase, she realizes that she feels slighted and disrespected by the host and offended that her husband hasn't objected to the proffered table. She interprets these emotions as threats to her personal sense of value; she must not be important enough or look nice enough to get a good table.

As a result of the analysis phase, she notices that her initial reaction is to act miffed and not talk to her husband since he didn't ask for a better table. She recognizes that this will likely confuse him and make him unpleasant during dinner, which will make her even more unhappy. She quickly identifies these outcomes as not the most positive for all concerned.

During the choice phase, she decides that her preferred outcome is to sit at a better table while eating a nice meal and enjoying meaningful conversation with her husband. To attain that outcome, she executes a new script: she looks around the restaurant and sees another table at which she would prefer to sit. When their server arrives, the teacher smiles and says, "I'm so sorry to cause any trouble, but this table is just too noisy for me. Is there another table available, perhaps that one?" as she points to her desired table. The server smiles back and goes to check, returning a few minutes later to inform them that while the selected table is taken, another table in a quieter corner of the restaurant is available. The teacher and her husband are escorted to the new table and enjoy their meal much more than they would have at the first table.

## Cultivating Satisfaction

In this book, we have emphasized the destructive nature of negative emotions and negative patterns of thought. A logical conclusion would be that we should constantly seek out positive emotions like happiness, joy, or even euphoria. While it is true that positive emotions have benefits, they do not constitute a viable long-term goal for those seeking to optimize the inner world. This is because positive emotions, as pleasant as they can be, are still emotions and will fade as soon as the effects of the chemicals that produce them (for example, dopamine, serotonin, and glutamate) diminish. Again, positive emotions generate wonderful experiences for us, and they should be savored when they occur. However, for a more stable positive experience we should try to cultivate a long-term sense of satisfaction.

Using the work of Edward Deci and Richard Ryan (1987, 2008a, 2008b; Deci, 1995; Deci, Connell, & Ryan, 1989; Deci, Koestner, & Ryan, 1999; Ryan & Deci, 2000), we can operationalize the construct of satisfaction. Specifically, Deci (1995) identified critical features of a fully functioning individual. For Deci and his colleagues, fully functioning people are using their skills and abilities in ways that are personally meaningful and produce positive results for those with whom they interact. In our terms, fully functioning people are both self-actualized and connected to something greater than self. We prefer to replace the term *fully functioning* with the term *fully satisfied*, mainly because a fully functioning person, by definition, experiences life in a positive way (although he or she might not always be experiencing positive emotions). When trying to take care of ourselves, it is better to focus on long-term, stable outcomes as opposed to immediate but short-lived outcomes. Deci (1995) identified three characteristics of satisfied (that is, fully functioning) individuals: a sense of competence, a sense of autonomy, and a sense of relatedness.

A sense of *competence* or effectiveness is central to human satisfaction. In fact, Deci (1995) noted that this drive is linked to intrinsic motivation:

> Feeling competent at the task is an important aspect of one's intrinsic satisfaction. The feeling of being effective is satisfying in its own right, and can even represent the primary draw for a lifelong career. People realize that the more they invest in a job, the better they will get at it, and thus the more intrinsic satisfaction they will experience. (p. 64)

Deci further explained:

> The feeling of competency results when a person takes on and, in his or her own view, meets optimal challenges. Optimal challenge is a key concept here. Being able to do something that is trivially easy does not lead to perceived competence, for the feeling of being effective occurs spontaneously only when one has worked toward accomplishment. . . . All of us are striving for mastery, for affirmations of our own competence. One does not have to be best or first, or to get an "A," to feel competent; one need only take on a meaningful personal challenge and give it one's best. (p. 66)

The second trait of people who are fully satisfied is that they operate from a sense of *autonomy* or freedom. As Deci (1995) noted:

> People who were asked to do a particular task but allowed the freedom of having some say in how to do it were more

> fully engaged by the activity—they enjoyed it more—than people who were not treated as unique individuals. (pp. 33–34)

Of course, we cannot always operate with complete autonomy or freedom. However, we can look for opportunities for autonomy or freedom even within the constraints in our lives. Additionally, we can seek out life experiences that maximize our freedom and autonomy.

The third trait of satisfied people is relatedness. *Relatedness* means being connected to other human beings. At first it might appear that the trait of relatedness might be inconsistent with the trait of autonomy or freedom. Deci (1995) reconciled this issue as follows:

> People have often portrayed the needs for autonomy and relatedness as being implicitly contradictory. You have to give up your autonomy, they say, to be related to others. But that is simply a misportrayal of the human being. Part of the confusion stems from equating autonomy and independence, which are in fact very different concepts. Independence means to do for yourself, to *not* rely on others for personal nourishment and emotional support. Autonomy, in contrast, means to act freely, with a sense of volition and choice. It is thus possible for a person to be independent and autonomous (i.e., to freely not rely on others), or to be independent and controlled (i.e., to feel forced not to rely on others). (pp. 88–89)

We believe that teaching is a profession that is almost perfectly designed for human satisfaction as defined by Deci's three characteristics. Relative to competence or effectiveness, teaching is one of the most complex professions in which one can engage. Thus, it provides a lifetime of opportunities to increase one's sense of competence. As teachers get better at the myriad of challenging tasks confronting them daily, they develop a stronger and stronger sense of competence. Relative to autonomy or freedom, teaching allows for a great deal of individuality. Although teachers have specific content they must teach and even specific instructional strategies they must employ, they have great autonomy and freedom regarding how they approach content and execute strategies. Relative to relatedness, teaching, by definition, allows for making connections with other human beings. Every student represents an opportunity to connect deeply to and positively influence another person. Teaching might offer more opportunities for connectedness than the vast majority of other vocations. In effect, to be fully satisfied, teachers need only look to their chosen profession. Mastery of that profession will pay great dividends in personal reward.

# Identifying and Living From Our Ideals

In chapter 4, we saw that our ideals represent those beliefs about the nature of the world that we would like to be true. When we have evidence that those beliefs are in fact true, we are inspired. Of course, such ideals could be quite different from person to person. Certainly, in this book, we would not presume to offer a list of important ideals to live from. However, there are some broad categories of ideals that most probably relate to the vast majority of people in the teaching profession. Here, we address two categories of ideals identified by Southwick and Charney (2012) as characteristics of resilient people: moral purpose and altruism.

## Moral Purpose

Southwick and Charney (2012) contended that people who exhibit resiliency also demonstrate a strong sense of moral purpose, which they refer to as "doing the right thing." They noted, "In our interviews, we found that many resilient individuals possessed a keen sense of right and wrong that strengthened them during periods of extreme stress and afterward, as they adjusted to life following trauma" (p. 64). Southwick and Charney warned that following a moral purpose or one's "moral compass" (p. 64) takes courage because when we stand for something we value, we will likely meet with resistance. It is when we meet resistance that we require courage. They provided extreme examples like the resistance encountered by Senator John McCain and James Bond Stockdale when imprisoned in the "Hanoi Hilton" during the Vietnam War. They and others faced unspeakable physical and psychological torture when they stood up for what they believed was right—in this case, they refused to reveal military secrets or comply with enemy demands.

Obviously, we must be very sure about our values and beliefs to exhibit such convictions. To this end, Southwick and Charney (2012) recommended the work of Rushworth M. Kidder (2005) in his book, *Moral Courage*. Kidder outlined a three-step process. The first step is a candid self-analysis which entails asking questions like, What are my values and beliefs? Which are the most important to me? Am I living by these principles and values? Am I falling short, and where? Am I motivated to change? Do I have the courage to do so? The second step is to discuss our answers to these questions with someone whose morals we respect. As Southwick and Charney explained, "These discussions can then help me to recognize and analyze the numerous situations in life where my actions have moral implications, and to honestly evaluate the risks and dangers involved in defending my core values" (p. 78). The third step is to practice our moral values, recognize situations in which they might apply, and ensure that we do not shrink from the challenge. Southwick and Charney cited the work of Gus Lee (2006) in his book *Courage: The Backbone of Leadership*, in which he asserted that we must avoid being "seduced by avoidance" (p. 21). In his book *Why Courage Matters*, Senator John McCain (2004) went a step further, noting that there is no need to search for situations that require moral courage because these situations surround each of us every day of our lives.

## Altruism

According to Southwick and Charney (2012), altruism is "concern for the welfare of others, and giving to others with no expectation of [personal] benefit" (p. 64). Of course, people perform altruistic acts on a daily basis. Some are quite spectacular and are reported in the news. For example, consider Wesley Autrey. He was waiting for a train in New York City at the 137th Street subway station. A man standing on the platform collapsed and fell on the tracks right into the path of an oncoming train. In a split-second decision, Autrey jumped on the tracks and covered the fallen man with his own body. Amazingly, the train passed over both Autrey and the fallen man he was shielding, causing no bodily harm to either of the two (Buckley, 2007). About acts of altruism, Southwick and Charney noted:

> Heroic acts like that of Mr. Autrey, where one individual makes a sacrifice or takes a risk for the benefit of another, are examples of altruism. Social science research has shown that altruism is associated with resilience, positive mental health and well-being in people with and without mental disorders. (2012, p. 74)

They cited research from a new field of study called neuroethics. Neuroscientists examine how the brain processes moral and ethical thinking and decision making. The central question in their studies is, Are moral and ethical values hardwired into us? Apparently, the tentative answer is a qualified yes. Southwick and Charney explained:

> This research has found that mutual cooperation consistently activates brain regions (e.g. the dopamine nucleus accumbens system) that are known to be involved in the processing of reward. Thus, it appears that mutual cooperation, but not selfish behavior, tends to activate dopamine reward systems, which may leave the individual feeling good and wanting to repeat similar cooperative behaviors. Perhaps, through natural selection, the survival value of co-operation and group cohesion have been reinforced by the rewarding activation of dopamine systems. (2012, p. 76)

Altruistic behavior does not have to be as dramatic as the heroic act of Wesley Autrey. In fact, most acts of altruism are small acts of kindness that produce small but appreciated benefits for others. Here we provide a few examples:

*Joey Prusak: As the manager of a Dairy Queen in Minneapolis, Joey regularly took customers' orders. One day, after giving a visually impaired man his change, Joey noticed that the man dropped a twenty-dollar bill on the floor as he was putting his change into his pocket. A woman standing in line picked up the bill, but instead of returning it to the visually impaired man, she put it in her purse. Joey confronted the woman, asking her to return the money to its rightful owner. When the woman refused, Joey refused to serve her unless she returned the money. When the woman persisted in claiming that the money was her own, Joey took twenty dollars out of his own wallet and gave it to the visually impaired man. Of the incident, Joey said, "I was just doing what I thought was right. . . . I did it without even really thinking about it. . . . Ninety-nine out of one hundred people would've done the same thing as me." (Associated Press, 2013)*

*Baytown Fire Fighters: John McCormick was mowing his lawn one day when he suffered a heart attack. His family called 911, and an ambulance and firefighting crew responded. McCormick was taken to the hospital in the ambulance and, per standard procedure, the firefighting crew followed the ambulance in their truck. However, once they left the hospital, the firefighting crew decided not to head straight back to the fire station. Instead, they went back to McCormick's house, finished mowing his front lawn, mowed his back lawn, put the lawnmower in the garage, and left the key in the mailbox. One firefighter, Lt. J. D. Giles, left a note for John's wife, Patsy: "We felt bad that your husband didn't get to finish the yard, so we did." Of his crew's action, Giles said it wasn't a big deal: "Just something to help someone out in the worst time of their life." (Reece, 2014)*

*Mark Bustos: As a hair stylist in New York City, Mark spends his time helping people feel better about how they look. Sometimes he does it to earn a paycheck, but on Sundays—his only day off—he offers free haircuts and food to homeless people in his community. Mark says, "I do believe that people with a proper, professional haircut receive more respect than those who do not have a proper haircut." In response to his new look, one homeless man immediately asked Mark if he knew anyone who was hiring. Of his actions, Mark says, "I just simply wanted to bring some positive energy and hope into this world. . . . If we all do one random act of kindness daily, we just might set the world in the right direction." (Gamble, 2014)*

*Freshman in Delton, Michigan: A high school freshman student noticed that one of his classmates had worn the same clothes to school every day since school started. One day, the student saw that his classmate had torn his only shirt. So that night, the student went home and filled a backpack with extra clothes. He left it at the school office the next morning with a note asking that it be delivered to his classmate during the day. Eventually, people in the school and community heard about the anonymous donation and began bringing gently used or new clothes to the school to be given away to those in need. The collection of free clothes, dubbed "The We've Got Your Back Shack," expanded so quickly that it outgrew several locations throughout the school before moving to the school's basement and finally into its own building on campus. ("Boy's random act of kindness spreads through community," 2014)*

Altruism is available to each of us, probably on a weekly if not daily basis. All that we need to do is recognize the opportunities that present themselves and act on them.

# Implications for Daily Life

This chapter has laid out an ambitious scope of practices that teachers can use both in and out of the classroom. That work can begin with an analysis of our mental health in various aspects of our lives such as career, family relationships, and so on. If we conclude that we are not at a mentally healthy level in any of these areas, we examine where we might have obstacles using the hierarchy of needs. In addition to this self-analysis, we can use the three management phases (awareness, analysis, and choice) in our personal lives in a manner similar to their use in teaching (as discussed in chapter 1). We might practice these phases retrospectively or use them in real time when we become upset with specific people, events, or tasks. To take care of ourselves, we might also seek to develop a sense of satisfaction by working on Deci's three traits in the context of our teaching career: a sense of competence, autonomy, and relatedness. Finally, our long-term work on ourselves should also focus on identifying and fostering our ideals. Although ideals may be different from person to person, fostering a moral compass and engaging in acts of altruism are beneficial to everyone. The management process, a sense of satisfaction, and identification of ideals apply directly to the classroom context, and the general improvement of mental health in daily life can have an indirect effect as well.

# Chapter 6

## *Teaching With the Self–System in Mind*

The previous chapters detailed what teachers should know about the inner workings of their self-systems so that they might function more purposefully and effectively in their professional and personal lives. In addition to understanding the self-system for their own edification, teachers can use this understanding to enhance the lives of their students. This chapter addresses strategies and activities to this end. More pointedly, it addresses how to teach in such a way as to honor the self-system of each student who comes under our tutelage. With this perspective in mind, we consider the six levels of goals and desired states that constitute the self-system.

## Physiology and Safety

Levels 1 and 2 of the hierarchy of goals and desired states deal with physiological comfort and safety, respectively. As we have seen, if students don't have physiological comfort and feel safe, they will not be able to concentrate in class. Rather, their attention and energy will be focused on getting their basic needs met.

In general, U.S. schools have done a good job ensuring physiological comfort. Classrooms are warm in the winter and cool in the summer. Students are provided food and nourishment when their home environments do not afford these basics. This notwithstanding, it is useful to be aware of students' needs regarding physiology. A checklist like the following might serve to keep us cognizant of potential issues for specific students.

☐ The student has adequate food.

☐ The student's food provides him or her with adequate nutrition.

☐ The student has adequate clothing.

☐ The student's clothing provides adequate warmth.

☐ The student has adequate housing.

☐ The student's housing provides adequate protection.

☐ The student has the resources necessary to maintain an adequate level of personal hygiene.

☐ The student gets adequate exercise each day.

☐ The student has time to play each day.

☐ The student gets enough sleep each night.

☐ The student has access to medical care.

☐ The student has access to psychological care.

Physical safety is the second level of the hierarchy. Obviously, if students don't feel safe in class, they will be greatly distracted. U.S. schools do a fairly good job of keeping students safe, even though there is general sentiment to the contrary. That is, given the occurrence of horrific incidents at Heath High School in 1997, Westside Middle School in 1998, Columbine High School in 1999, Red Lake High School in 2005, Sandy Hook Elementary School in 2012, and others, some in the general public have developed the perception that schools are unsafe. The facts provide a different perspective. As reported by the National Center for Education Statistics (Kena et al., 2014), rates of nonfatal victimizations (theft, simple assault, rape, sexual assault, robbery, and aggravated assault) for twelve- to eighteen-year-old students have steadily declined over the past two decades, falling from 181 victimizations per 1,000 students in 1992 to 52 victimizations per 1,000 students in 2012. During the same time period, school-associated violent deaths have also declined from 57 during the 1992–1993 school year to 31 during the 2011–2012 school year (Robers, Kemp, & Truman, 2013; note that these data do not include tragedies that occurred after the 2011–2012 school year, such as the shooting in Newtown, Connecticut, in December 2012).

While the research does indicate that schools are relatively safe, such research does little to assuage the fears of some students. Scott and Marzano (2014) provided an interesting perspective. They cited evidence that tens of thousands of students skip school each day out of fear for their well-being. Tens of thousands bring weapons to school to protect themselves. Only a relatively small percentage of students report that they feel safe at school. Regardless of the facts about school safety, perceptions are what count within the self-system. With this in mind, it is useful to consider the following checklist regarding safety.

☐ The school building is well maintained with no signs of neglect or disrepair.

☐ Access to school grounds is limited (for example, the school grounds are fenced or walled).

☐ Visitors enter the school grounds/main building through one clearly marked entrance which is visible from the main office.

☐ Signs direct visitors to report to the main office upon entering the school, where they are given I.D. cards or badges to identify them as visitors.

☐ All staff wear clearly displayed I.D. cards or badges while on school grounds.

☐ Bus loading and drop-off zones are clearly defined and monitored when in use.

☐ Car drop-off and pick-up areas are clearly defined and monitored when in use.

☐ School buildings, shrubs, and trees are strategically located to ensure and preserve good sight lines on school grounds.

☐ There is adequate lighting around school buildings and on school grounds.

☐ Restricted areas of school buildings or grounds are clearly identified with appropriate signage.

☐ Written regulations exist and are enforced regarding student access to school grounds and buildings.

☐ Hallways and bathrooms are supervised by staff.

☐ Classrooms are locked when not in use.

☐ The school has an alarm system, and/or school grounds are monitored by security personnel outside of school hours.

☐ The school intercom system broadcasts indoors and outdoors to alert all students and staff to emergency situations.

☐ Emergency procedures for various situations (severe weather, earthquake, violent intruder, and so on) are clearly defined and practiced regularly.

☐ The school has a working relationship with local law enforcement authorities.

# Belonging and Esteem

A sense of belonging and a sense of esteem within a community are levels three and four, respectively, in the hierarchy. Both of these levels deal with our perceptions of relationships with others. There are a number of resources available to teachers regarding strategies that directly address students' perceptions of belonging and esteem within the classroom.

- *Creating Physical and Emotional Security in Schools* (Williams, 2012)
- *Motivating Students: 25 Strategies to Light the Fire of Engagement* (Chapman & Vagle, 2011)
- *You've Got to Reach Them to Teach Them: Hard Facts About the Soft Skills of Student Engagement* (Schreck, 2011)

- *The Best Schools: How Human Development Research Should Inform Educational Practice* (Armstrong, 2006)
- *Transforming Schools: Creating a Culture of Continuous Improvement* (Zmuda, Kuklis, & Kline, 2004)
- *The Respectful School: How Educators and Students Can Conquer Hate and Harassment* (Wessler, 2003)
- *Building Learning Communities With Character: How to Integrate Academic, Social, and Emotional Learning* (Novick, Kress, & Elias, 2002)
- *The Soul of Education: Helping Students Find Connection, Compassion, and Character at School* (Kessler, 2000)

We also recommend the book *The Highly Engaged Classroom* (Marzano & Pickering, 2011), which contains a wide range of specific strategies. Table 6.1 summarizes a few general strategies that address belonging and esteem.

**Table 6.1: Classroom Strategies to Address Belonging and Esteem**

| Strategy | Description |
|---|---|
| Fair and Equitable Treatment of All Students | Let all students know that the teacher is available and will provide help to any student in need. Curb disruptive, disrespectful, or hurtful behavior and actively encourage behavior that demonstrates respect. For example, establish a set of basic classroom rights, such as "All students and teachers have the right to be treated with respect." |
| Simple Courtesies | Greet students at the door, calling them by their names and making eye contact. As appropriate, share jokes or funny anecdotes with students or congratulate them on recent successes. |

Continued →

| Strategy | Description |
|---|---|
| **Physical Contact and Gestures** | Build a sense of belonging and esteem for students through physical contact, such as giving a student a pat on the back. Physical contact should always be used with attention to each student's age, gender, and culture. What may seem appropriate with one student might be inappropriate for another. Physical gestures (such as the "okay" hand signal, a thumbs-up, a wink, a nod, or a smile) can also communicate esteem for students. |
| **Students' Needs and Concerns** | Although attending to certain student needs is required by law (such as providing extra support to students with poor eyesight or learning disabilities), create an environment of belonging and esteem by taking note of and making accommodations for more personal needs that students might have. For example, a student who has missed school because of a serious illness or death in the family might need a bit of extra support to catch up. A student who joins the class in the middle of the year might need some tutoring and emotional support to feel like they fit in with the rest of the class. |
| **Positive Information About Students** | Identify something positive about each of your students and use that information to plan instruction that aligns with students' interests. If students have discipline issues or simply appear alienated from the rest of the class, use positive information to create structured opportunities in class for those students to share about themselves and their accomplishments. |

# Self-Actualization and Connection to Something Greater Than Self

As the previous discussion illustrates, the first four levels of the self-system hierarchy are common fare in K–12 education, although we should continue to improve our effectiveness at meeting students' needs in these areas. The last two levels of the hierarchy are not commonly an explicit emphasis in K–12 schooling.

The hierarchy levels of self-actualization and connection to something greater than self are interconnected in that they deal with hopes, dreams, and aspirations of students. To teach with self-actualization in mind, we must establish activities that allow students to set goals that are of personal interest to them, and then encourage them to work toward the accomplishment of those goals. There are a number of things you can do in the classroom to facilitate students' setting personal goals.

## Possible Selves

To ensure that students set goals big enough to excite them, it is useful to introduce them to the concept of possible selves. Researchers Hazel Markus and Paula Nurius (1986) described possible selves in the following way:

> Possible selves are represented in the same way as the here-and-now self (imaginal, semantic) and can be viewed as cognitive bridges between the present and future, specifying how individuals may change from how they are now to what they will become. (p. 961)

We create versions of our possible selves by a direct comparison to those people we encounter in our lives. As Markus and Nurius explained, our possible selves "are the direct result of previous social comparisons in which the individual's own thoughts, feelings, characteristics, and behaviors have been contrasted to those of salient others. What others are now, I could become" (p. 954).

Possible selves are the way we explore what we might be, using both positive and negative scenarios. The fact that possible selves are not always positive is not a negative situation. Indeed, when we imagine negative possible selves, it allows us to examine and choose between a variety of options. As Susan Harter explained (1999):

> It is most desirable to have a balance between positive ex-
> pected selves and negative feared selves, so that positive
> possible selves (e.g., obtaining a well-paying job, wanting
> to be loved by family, hoping to be recognized and ad-
> mired by others) can give direction to desired future states,
> whereas negative possible selves (e.g., being unemployed,
> feeling lonely, being socially ignored) can clarify what is to
> be avoided. (p. 146)

Teachers can directly present students with the concept of possible selves through discussion and personal examples. Once an initial awareness of the construct has been established, Daphna Oyserman, Kathy Terry, and Deborah Bybee (2002) recommended the activities shown in table 6.2.

**Table 6.2: Activities to Promote Awareness of Possible Selves**

| Activity | Description |
|---|---|
| **Accomplishment Introductions** | Ask students to introduce themselves in a way that indicates something they would like to accomplish someday. For example, students might think of a person who has accomplished something similar to their goal and then introduce themselves using their first name and the last name of the person they thought of. If a student named Jake wanted to be a star football quarterback someday, he might introduce himself as Jake Manning (in recognition of Peyton Manning, the star football quarterback for the Denver Broncos). |
| **Life Images** | Ask students to find pictures of individuals doing various activities related to school, work, family, lifestyle, community service, health, and hobbies. For example, students might search in magazines or online for pictures of people engaging in specific fitness activities that they prefer to engage in to stay healthy. |

| Activity | Description |
|---|---|
| **Timelines** | Have students create timelines for their futures. Ask them to think about what they would like to do, accomplish, and be as far into the future as possible. Ask that they think specifically about important choices they may have to make, roadblocks they might encounter that could change the direction of their lives, or circumstances that they will encounter as they work toward their goals. |
| **Possible Selves Research** | Ask students to find information about what is required to become their possible selves. A student who wants to become a restaurant owner and chef might research how to operate a successful business, which culinary schools are best for the type of cuisine he would like to focus on, and how to get started (for example, by starting with a food truck and eventually moving into a restaurant space). |
| **Informational Interviews** | Help students contact adults in their communities who have accomplished or achieved goals similar to those the students want to achieve. For example, a student who wants to run her own business someday might use a list of women-owned businesses to find individuals who can advise her about her journey. |

## The Growth Mindset

Along with exploring their future possible selves, students might be asked to examine their mindsets. Carol Dweck (2000) made this concept popular in her book *Self-Theories*. She and her colleagues found that relatively early in life, we develop one of two theories about ourselves as to why we succeed or fail in certain situations. One theory is referred to as the *fixed mindset*. The other theory is referred to as the *growth mindset*. If we subscribe to the fixed mindset, we believe that native ability or intelligence accounts for our success or lack thereof. If we are successful at something, it is because we possess ability or native intelligence in that area. If we are not successful at something, it is because we don't have ability or native intelligence in that area.

The growth mindset provides a very different perspective on success or failure. As opposed to crediting an outcome to ability or intelligence, we ascribe it to the amount of effort we are willing to expend. Stated simply, we take the position that we can be successful at the vast majority of situations that come our way if we are willing to expend the right amount of effort.

Not surprisingly, we approach difficult tasks quite differently depending on our mindset. If we have a fixed mindset, we tend to shy away from those tasks we perceive as difficult. After all, if it is arduous for us to do then we probably don't have the requisite ability or intelligence. If we have the growth mindset, we are not deterred by the perceived difficulty of a task. If it is something in which we are interested, we simply increase our level of effort to account for the increased level of difficulty.

Dweck (2000) noted that one of the more interesting aspects of our mindsets is that they are not necessarily permanent. Those with a fixed mindset can become aware of its limitations and can engage in activities to cultivate a growth mindset. To this end, Marzano and Heflebower (2012) recommended that teachers introduce students to the two types of mindsets. Teachers can present and discuss the characteristics of the two types of mindsets. It is also useful and important to provide students with clear examples of the growth mindset, like the following:

*Pitcher Maury Wills loved baseball. He loved the thrill of staring down a batter with a full count and hearing the umpire call, "Strike three, you're out!" He was a great fielder too, with quick reflexes and excellent catching and throwing skills. He knew he was good at these things. However, batting was a big problem for him. He couldn't hit anything! Nevertheless, the Dodgers signed him to their minor league team, and Wills hoped he would improve his hitting skills. He practiced hitting baseballs for hours every day, and even learned to be a switch hitter (hitting both right- and left-handed). After eight long years in the minors, Wills finally got his chance to play with the major league team. But he still faltered when he went to bat. Fortunately, Wills's first-base coach recognized that his problem was more mental than physical; Wills just didn't believe that he was a good hitter. With his coach's help, Wills changed his patterns of thinking about himself as a hitter and, as a result, saw dramatic improvement in his performance at the plate. He broke Ty Cobb's record for stolen bases during his first season in the majors and eventually earned a spot in baseball's Hall of Fame (Kersey, 1998).*

Once students have a general awareness of the two types of mindsets, teachers can provide them with a more detailed listing of characteristics of the two theories. Table 6.3 (page 106) offers such a listing.

Teachers can discuss these various traits of the fixed versus growth mindsets and invite students to engage in a private inventory of their own tendencies. Students can use the brief reflection log in table 6.4 (page 107) to this end. Inventories like those in table 6.4 serve the same purpose as Seligman's (2006) self-analysis system to determine an optimistic versus pessimistic explanatory style. In fact, we believe that older students can use either Seligman's or Dweck's (2000) approach with similar results. However, Dweck's two mindsets appear more easily adaptable to younger students.

**Table 6.3: Characteristics of Fixed Versus Growth Mindsets**

| Fixed | Growth |
|---|---|
| You believe there are some subjects in school at which you are very good, and some subjects at which you are very poor. | You believe that the subjects in school at which you do well are the ones at which you try the hardest, and the subjects at which you do poorly are the ones into which you don't put a lot of effort. |
| You believe it is never okay to fail at something. | You believe that failing at something can teach you what you need to improve on. |
| You believe that it is important to know how likely you are to succeed at something before you take it on. | You believe that being interested in something is reason enough to try hard at it. |
| You believe that people cannot change their basic personalities. | You believe that people can change almost anything about themselves. |
| You believe that people don't have much control over what happens to them. | You believe that people can control most things in their lives. |
| You believe that negative things have happened in your life that you cannot overcome. | You believe that negative things that have happened in your life can serve to make you a better person if you try to learn from them. |

## Table 6.4: Student Reflection Log

| Fixed Mindset |
| --- |
| I have a fixed mindset about: |
| How I feel when I'm engaged in this: |
| What I say to myself when I'm engaged in this: |
| How and why I developed this mindset: |
| Things I can do to change this mindset: |

| Growth Mindset |
| --- |
| I have a growth mindset about: |
| How I feel when I'm engaged in this: |
| What I say to myself when I'm engaged in this: |
| How and why I developed this mindset: |
| Things I can do to support this mindset: |

*Visit* **marzanoresearch.com/reproducibles** *for a reproducible version of this table.*

## Dispositions for Success

Closely related to the growth mindset is the concept of mental dispositions that breed success. Indeed, well before the concept of mindsets became popular, mental dispositions were discussed as a critical aspect of K–12 instruction (see Marzano et al., 1988). Arthur Costa and Bena Kallick (2014) described dispositions in the following way:

> A disposition is a habit, a preparation, a state of readiness, or a tendency to act in a specified way. When we use the term "dispositions," we are referring to *thinking dispositions*—tendencies toward particular patterns of intellectual behavior. (p. 19)

A disposition might be thought of as a rule we have developed about success. It is a part of our "theory of the world," as described in chapter 4. Marzano and Heflebower (2012) discussed three thinking dispositions that serve to augment the growth mindset and help students effectively engage in self-actualizing activities.

1. **Staying focused even when answers or solutions are not immediately apparent:** This disposition relates to the growth mindset in that it is focused on effort. Few things of consequence come easily. Indeed, most significant accomplishments manifest only after prolonged periods of failure and intervals of time when solutions and answers seemed unattainable. To make students aware of this disposition, Marzano and Heflebower (2012) recommend frank discussions ideally involving real-life personal examples from the teacher in which the disposition was employed and examples in which the disposition was not employed. For example, a teacher might describe a time in his life when he was enrolled in a physics class that was particularly challenging for him. Try as he might, he simply couldn't acquire the basic understanding of physics principles necessary to do well on the homework and quizzes. He ended up dropping out of the course after the first four weeks. The teacher further explains that to this very day he regrets having done

this, because he now realizes that his success was simply a matter of hanging on a little while longer. In addition to personal anecdotes, the teacher might also present stories like the following:

*James Cameron:* *Cameron grew up in a small town in Canada. When he was fifteen, he saw Stanley Kubrick's film* 2001: A Space Odyssey *and immediately knew he wanted to be a filmmaker. However, he was just a young kid in a small town in Canada; how could he become a filmmaker? Nevertheless, Cameron worked hard to figure out how to make movies and create special effects, experimenting with his father's Super 8 camera. In time, because of his father's job, Cameron's family moved to Orange County in California, near Hollywood, but since Cameron didn't have a driver's license, Hollywood was still out of reach for him. After realizing that he didn't want to study physics or English in college, Cameron and two of his friends wrote a ten-minute script and raised enough money to rent a camera, lenses, film stocks, and a studio. At first, they couldn't figure out how to work the camera and spent half of their first day just trying to get it running. Cameron had no one to teach him about special effects, so he went to the library of the University of Southern California and read graduate theses about optical printing, front screen projection, dye transfers, and anything else that might be helpful. Eventually, Cameron got the opportunity to direct a film, but when he showed up to his first day on the shoot, he discovered that his entire crew was Italian and spoke no English. Cameron was fired three weeks later because the producer of the film didn't like his work. Nevertheless, Cameron persisted and wrote a script for a movie about a robotic hit man sent from the future to kill someone, which eventually became the popular film,* The Terminator. *Cameron has since directed many extremely successful movies such as* Aliens, Titanic, *and* Avatar. *(James Cameron Online, n.d.)*

*Tom Monaghan: When Monaghan was only four, his father died. His mother wasn't able to care for her children, so Monaghan spent most of his youth in and out of foster homes and orphanages. He wanted to be a priest, but got expelled from seminary for pillow fighting and talking in chapel. He returned to school and graduated last in his class. He wanted to study architecture at the University of Michigan, but he didn't have the grades or the money to make it happen. He enlisted in the Marine Corps and managed to save $2,000, but fell for a "get-rich-quick" scheme, lost it all, and found himself stranded in San Diego. After hitchhiking home, Monaghan and his brother borrowed $900 and bought a tiny pizza store. Eight months in, Monaghan's brother got tired of the venture and traded his share in the business for Monaghan's Volkswagen Beetle. Monaghan continued in the business, working one hundred hours a week or more, simplifying the menu, limiting the sizes and toppings available, and setting high standards for ingredients. He also decided to offer pizza delivery in thirty minutes or less. He said, "It didn't make sense to use only the best ingredients if the pizza was cold and tasteless when the customer got it." As Monaghan's business grew, he bought more stores, eventually selling franchises and figuring out that college towns were excellent spots for stores. He renamed his stores Domino's Pizza and set the ambitious goal of opening one new store per week. However, expanding so rapidly was a disaster, and Monaghan found himself in debt to the tune of $1.5 million dollars with a horde of failing stores. He reset his goal to twenty new stores per year and began monitoring each store more carefully. This strategy proved successful, and Domino's opened its 1,000th franchise in 1983, an occasion that Monaghan celebrated by buying the Detroit Tigers baseball team. In 1998, he sold his stake in the company for $1 billion dollars. Unfortunately, a survey in 2009 found that Domino's pizza came in last among consumer taste preferences. In response, Domino's launched a new ad campaign in which they showed people criticizing their pizza, and then introduced chefs*

who were recreating the pizza's taste profile to be fresher, more deli-
cious, and more appealing. The campaign seems to have been a success,
as Domino's experienced a historic 14.3 percent quarterly gain the following year. ("Tom Monaghan in 30 minutes or less," 2008)

2. **Pushing the limits of your knowledge and skills:**
   Cultivation of this disposition requires students to work
   outside their comfort zone for extended periods of time.
   This is not a typical way to approach tasks, particularly
   difficult ones. Indeed, we tend to select tasks which can be
   accomplished easily given our known skills and abilities,
   particularly if we have a fixed mindset. Again, students can
   be provided with real-life examples of this disposition:

*Jaymie Matthews: Matthews, a researcher at the University of British
Columbia, is an astroseismologist. That means he studies vibrations or
pulsations that shake stars. Studying such vibrations allows astrophys-
icists to glean information about the internal structures of stars, which
they can use to make inferences about the stars' size, mass, composition,
and age. Matthews wanted to detect tiny variations in the luminosity of
stars that typically indicate pulsations shaking the surface of the stars.
However, the Hubble Space Telescope didn't have the requisite sensitivity to accurately detect such variations. So, Matthews worked with the
Canadian Space Agency to design and build the MOST (Microvariability
and Oscillation of STars) space telescope. About the size and shape of a
large suitcase, the MOST telescope cost $10 million dollars to build (com-
pared to $2 billion for the Hubble Space Telescope) and detects variations
in star luminosity ten times better than the Hubble Space Telescope.
Discoveries made by Matthews and his team using their MOST telescope regularly make headlines. (ASTROLab, 2006)*

*Quincy Jones: Jones loved music from a young age and tried nearly every instrument in his school band before settling on the trumpet. As a teenager, he befriended a local singer and piano player named Ray Charles and played together with him before attending Berklee College of Music in Boston. However, he dropped out when an opportunity to tour with bandleader Lionel Hampton arose. Afterwards, Jones settled in New York and over the next decade worked with musicians such as Count Basie, Duke Ellington, Gene Krupa, Tommy Dorsey, and Dizzy Gillespie. However, Jones wanted to learn more. In 1957, he moved to Paris to study musical composition with Nadia Boulanger and Olivier Messiaen. He subsequently began writing scores for musicals, and in 1964 he landed a job as Vice President of Mercury Records—the first African American to hold an executive position in a Caucasian-owned record company. Determined to keep expanding his knowledge and skills, Jones turned his attention to writing film scores, eventually composing the scores for thirty-three major motion pictures. Jones continued to explore new areas, composing theme music for television series such as* Ironside, Sanford and Son, *and* The Bill Cosby Show. *In August of 1974, Jones almost died due to a cerebral aneurysm (burst blood vessels in the brain). Not to be slowed down though, Jones was back at work six months later and ready to face new challenges. Jones worked with pop star Michael Jackson to produce his first solo album,* Off the Wall, *and again in 1982 to produce* Thriller, *which became the best-selling album of all time (with over forty million copies sold). But even that wasn't enough for Jones. In 1985 he became a filmmaker, coproducing Steven Spielberg's adaptation of* The Color Purple. *Over the course of his life, Jones has won an Emmy award, seven Oscar nominations, and the Academy of Motion Picture Arts and Sciences Jean Hersholt Humanitarian Award, and he is the Grammy's all-time most nominated artist with a total of seventy-six nominations and twenty-six awards. (Academy of Achievement, 2010)*

3. **Generating, trusting, and maintaining your own standards of excellence:** This disposition requires students to think outside the proverbial box. It is probably one of the more difficult dispositions to cultivate because it goes against so many of our basic assumptions, namely that there are standards of excellence that have been established in any given field that we all should follow. While it is certainly true that standards of excellence are established and recognized in virtually every human endeavor, it is also true that challenging these standards can have profound effects on the results of a task. Some notable examples of the breakthroughs that have occurred because of people who have engaged this disposition include the following:

*Larry Page: Page, the CEO and founder of Google, isn't satisfied with improving his company's products by 10 percent, although many companies would be thrilled with that kind of improvement. Instead, Page expects his employees to offer services and create products that are ten times better than the competition, and he holds himself to the same high standard. At Stanford, his original thesis idea was to create a tool to annotate web pages—instead, he ended up creating a search engine (Google) that has changed the way people use the Internet. When Google decided to offer an email service, Page insisted that it offer users one hundred times the storage of competitors. Instead of translating selected works, Page led Google to create a translation service that would translate anything on the Internet from any language to any other language. Instead of offering users a library of recently published titles, Google set out to scan and index the contents of every book ever published. Google projects consistently reflect Page's "ten times better" mentality: a self-driving car, an artificial brain, and wearable computing systems like Google Glass. One of Page's employees, Astro Teller, described Page's mentality using a hypothetical story: Teller imagined wheeling a time machine into Page's office. Teller plugged it in and invited Page to travel to any time he'd like. The time machine worked! When Page returned from his adventures, he considered the time machine and asked Teller, "Does it have to plug in?*

*Why isn't it wireless? Wouldn't it be better if it didn't need power at all?" Teller explained that Page would act this way, not because he is disappointed with the time machine, but because "it's just core to who he is. There's always more to do, and his focus is on where the next 10X will come from." (Levy, 2013)*

---

***Warren Buffett:** Billionaire Warren Buffett has two rules for investing: (1) don't lose money, and (2) don't forget rule 1. He lives his personal life by these rules too. Although he is worth billions, Buffett is extremely frugal. He still lives in the Omaha home that he bought in 1958 for $31,500. He avoids buying "toys" or technology that require maintenance and further expense, seeing them as easy ways to lose money. He defines luxury and success as "really doing what you love and doing it well. It's as simple as that. Really getting to do what you love to do everyday—that's really the ultimate luxury." His salary of only $100,000 at Berkshire Hathaway reflects this definition. He enjoys what he does and finds greater value in doing his work well than in the monetary compensation he gets for it. (Smith, 2009)*

---

As was the case with the growth mindset, students can perform a self-audit on each of these dispositions. Table 6.5 includes a set of questions useful to this end.

Possible selves, the growth mindset, and dispositions of success are the tools human beings use to be self-actualized—to accomplish tasks that are important to them. Ultimately, if we are to teach in such a way that enhances self-actualization, then students must be allowed to work on projects of their own design.

**Table 6.5: Self-Analysis for Dispositions**

| Disposition: Staying Focused Even When Answers or Solutions Are Not Immediately Apparent |
| --- |
| A time when I did this was: |
| The outcome of my doing this was: |
| How I felt about myself: |
| Areas where I should use this disposition more: |
| **Disposition: Pushing the Limits of My Knowledge and Skills** |
| A time when I did this was: |
| The outcome of my doing this was: |
| How I felt about myself: |
| Areas where I should use this disposition more: |
| **Disposition: Generating, Trusting, and Maintaining My Own Standards of Excellence** |
| A time when I did this was: |
| The outcome of my doing this was: |
| How I felt about myself: |
| Areas where I should use this disposition more: |

*Visit* **marzanoresearch.com/reproducibles** *for a reproducible version of this table.*

## Personal Projects

Virtually all of the self-actualization strategies can be combined in what has been referred to as the "personal project" (Marzano & Pickering, 2011; Scott & Marzano, 2014). Specifically, personal projects are designed to provide students with opportunities to accomplish goals that are personally important to them. This, of course, gets right to the core of self-actualization—setting personal goals of import and working on them.

The idea of engaging students in projects of their own design is not new. Ken Macrorie (1988) employed this focus when he created the I-Search paper. When they write I-Search papers, students select topics of personal interest, research them, and write about them with a special emphasis on how the new information they have uncovered relates to their lives.

Another example of students engaging in projects of their own design is a *capstone project*. According to the Glossary of Education Reform (2014), a capstone project can be defined as follows:

> Also called a *capstone experience, culminating project,* or *senior exhibition,* among many other terms, a capstone project is a multifaceted assignment that serves as a culminating academic and intellectual experience for students, typically during their final year of high school or middle school, or at the end of an academic program or learning-pathway experience. While similar in some ways to a college thesis, capstone projects may take a wide variety of forms, but most are long-term investigative projects that culminate in a final product, presentation, or performance. For example, students may be asked to select a topic, profession, or social problem that interests them, conduct research on the subject, maintain a portfolio of findings or results, create a final product demonstrating their learning acquisition or conclusions (a paper, short film, or multimedia presentation, for example), and give an oral presentation on the project to a panel of teachers, experts, and community members who collectively evaluate its quality.

Here we present a version of a personal project specifically designed for K–12 classrooms. The rudiments of our version of the personal project are described in table 6.6.

**Table 6.6: The Personal Project**

| Phase | Description |
|---|---|
| **1. What Do I Want to Accomplish?** | A personal project begins with students selecting a personal goal. This goal should interest them and relate to a topic about which they are excited or passionate. One technique to help students select goals that truly inspire them is to pose the question, What would you do if you knew you would not fail? Of course, a discussion about world theories and ideals can accompany goal selection. Students might be reticent about sharing their beliefs because they are concerned about being teased or ridiculed. The best way to address this is for teachers to engage in their own personal projects alongside students and share their responses during each phase. Students may also hesitate to share their goals because they do not believe that they can accomplish them. Such a situation invites a discussion of growth mindsets versus fixed mindsets. |
| **2. Who Else Has Accomplished the Same Goal, and Who Will Support Me?** | The second phase focuses on students seeking heroes, role models, and mentors who will act as support systems as they pursue their individual goals from phase one. These individuals should be people who have accomplished goals similar to the ones students have identified. To accomplish this, students typically must conduct research and gather information about individuals who might be heroes, role models, and mentors. Teachers can make a distinction between mentors and heroes or role models by explaining that mentors are people with whom students can actually interact. Even if mentors have not accomplished the same goals toward which students are striving, they can be a source of encouragement. |

Continued →

| Phase | Description |
|---|---|
| **3. What Skills and Resources Will I Need to Accomplish My Goal?** | During phase three, students gather information about what is required to accomplish their goals. In contrast to phase one (where the focus is on thinking without fear of failure), phase three is focused on the hard facts regarding the accomplishment of a challenging goal. Students must determine the steps they will need to take to accomplish their goal and what information and skills they will need to implement those steps. |
| **4. What Will I Have to Change to Achieve My Goal?** | Of all the phases associated with personal projects, this one is the most challenging and confrontational because students must identify how their current behavior needs to change to accomplish their goals. Stated differently, students must confront scripts they have that are getting in their way. Willingness to change a personal behavior (that is, a script) that is not contributing to the achievement of one's goals is the centerpiece of all truly notable accomplishments. Teachers can facilitate this phase if they are willing to share their own scripts that get in the way of accomplishing their goals. |
| **5. What Is My Plan for Achieving My Goal, and How Hard Will I Have to Work?** | During the fifth phase, students write a concrete plan to accomplish their goals. This is a metacognitive function. The plan is a general outline for future actions and decisions, and students should recognize that they may need to make revisions to their plans as various circumstances and opportunities arise. Even so, plans should be as detailed as possible and should include milestones and significant events. Detailed plans help make goals and the actions associated with them clearer and more real in students' minds. |

| Phase | Description |
|---|---|
| **6. What Small Steps Can I Take Right Now?** | Phase six helps students identify things they can do immediately to set themselves on the path toward achieving their goals. These are referred to as short-term goals. Teachers can explain to students that accomplishing short-term goals that only take a few days or weeks can help them accomplish their long-term goals. In fact, accomplishing long-term goals can be defined as accomplishing a series of related short-term goals. As students set short-term goals (or small steps), they should write them down and give them to the teacher. The teacher then returns the goals to the student after the due date for the small step. |
| **7. How Have I Been Doing, and What Have I Learned About Myself?** | As students set and achieve short-term goals and evaluate whether or not they met those goals, the teacher can ask them to examine how well things are going and identify corrections they need to make in their behavior. Personal projects will eventually end (at least in terms of class time spent on them). When such a time comes, it is useful to ask students to reflect on what they have learned about themselves as a result of their personal project. Teachers should share the same. |

*Source: Adapted from Scott & Marzano, 2014.*

The personal project described in table 6.6 can be approached as a course in itself, or it can be embedded in an existing class or structure such as homeroom. Its central focus is students working on long-term goals they have selected. However, while students execute their personal projects, the teacher can reinforce the concept of possible selves by helping students articulate future versions of themselves that excite and motivate them. Personal projects also provide many opportunities to cultivate a growth mindset. Finally, as students encounter obstacles in their projects, they can practice the dispositions of success.

## Inspiration and Personal Values

The highest level of the hierarchy of goals and desired states introduced in chapter 2 is connection to something greater than self. While such connections are specific to individuals, there are some overt ways that teachers can help students identify those ideals to which they aspire. To this end, Robert J. Marzano and Debra J. Pickering (2011) recommended a systematic diet of inspirational stories like the following about Amy Purdy.

*Amy Purdy was a competitive snowboarder until she contracted bacterial meningitis at age nineteen, leading to the loss of her kidneys, her spleen, and both of her legs below the knee. As she recovered, Amy decided to turn her challenges and limitations into opportunities. She says, "I had to let go of the old Amy and learn to embrace the new Amy." To begin with, she focused on positive aspects of her new situation: she could be as tall as she wanted or as short as she wanted, her feet would never be cold again, and best of all, she could make her feet the size of all the shoes on the sale rack! She asked herself, "If my life were a book and I were the author, how would I want the story to go?" She imagined herself living the new life she wanted: walking gracefully, helping other people, and snowboarding again. She pictured herself snowboarding so vividly that she could feel the wind on her face and feel her heart beating faster as she carved down the mountain. In the face of setbacks—such as falling while snowboarding and watching her legs, still attached to her snowboard, continue down the mountain without her—Amy forced herself to get creative. When she couldn't find prosthetic legs that worked well with a snowboard, she designed her own new set of feet, ankles, and legs that would allow her the flexibility she needed to compete again. Amy also reached out to others facing the same obstacles; in 2005, she cofounded a nonprofit organization for youth and young adults with physical disabilities who want to be involved in action sports. Wearing her new legs, she won two World Cup medals (gold and bronze) in 2011, making her the highest-ranked adaptive female snowboarder in the world. In 2014, Amy won a bronze medal in the Sochi Paralympics and was a finalist on the popular television show,* Dancing With the Stars. *Of her experiences, Amy says, "In our minds we can do anything and we can be anything. It's believing in those dreams and facing our fears head-on that allows us to live our lives beyond our limits. . . . Instead of looking at our challenges and our limitations as something negative or bad, we can begin to look at them as blessings, magnificent gifts that can be used to ignite our imaginations and help us go further than we ever knew we could go." (Purdy, 2011)*

Marzano and Pickering (2011) also recommended showing students inspirational films in part or in their entirety, such as *Rudy, A Beautiful Mind, October Sky, Oliver Twist, Mr. Holland's Opus, The Pursuit of Happyness, Apollo 13, Babe, Miracle,* and *Glory.* Such films and stories can and should be used systematically. A teacher might schedule the viewing of part of a film or the reading of a short story every week, and provide time for students to discuss how the contents of the film or story relate to their personal views of the world.

While inspirational films and stories can provide students with an awareness that they have ideals to which they can aspire, a very direct approach is to ask them to articulate their ideals. Such activities should occur only when students are developmentally ready. Figure 6.1 provides one student's response to an assignment in which students in a high school class were asked to describe their personal ethics or ideals.

Ethics vary with environment, circumstances, and culture. In my own life, ethics play a major role. Whether it was because of the way I was raised, the experiences I've had, or just my outlook on the world and the way things should be. My biggest aspects of ethics include being honest, compassionate, and looking for the best and beauty in everyone.

I have been told repeatedly that I trust people too easily, but I find that when I put my faith and trust in people when others would not dare to, they almost never betray me. I would hope that people would put that same faith in me. Trust and honesty is an investment you put in people; if you build enough trust in them and show yourself to be honest, they will do the same in you. I value honesty so much, and it is an expectation I have of myself. I will put honesty before the risk of humiliation, before selfishness, and before anything less worthy of the Gospel truth. Even in being honest and trust worthy, I do not come off cold and heartless. Compassion and honesty go hand in hand, if enough of each is put into every situation. I admire those who trust and are trust worthy.

Compassion is the greatest form of love humans have to offer. According to Webster's Dictionary compassion means a feeling of sympathy for another's misfortune. My definition of compassion is forgiving, loving, helping, leading, and showing mercy for others. I have this theory that if one person can go out of their way to show compassion, then it will start a chain reaction of the same. People will never know how far a little kindness can go.

It wasn't until recently that I learned that the first and the second and the third impressions can be deceitful of what kind of person someone is. For example, imagine you had just met someone, and you speak with them three times on brief everyday conversations. They come off as a harsh, cruel, stubborn, and ignorant person. You reach your judgment based on just these three encounters. Let me ask you something . . . did you ever ask them what their goal in life is, what kind of past they came from, did they experience love, did they experience hurt, did you look into their soul and not just at their appearance? Until you know them and not just their "type," you have no right to shun them. You have not looked for their beauty, their good. You have not seen the light in their eyes. Look hard enough and you will always find a light, and you can even help it grow, if you don't walk away from those three impressions first.

I am sure that my codes of life may be very different from yours, but how do you know that trust, compassion, and beauty will not make this world a better place to be in and this life a better one to live? My codes may seem like a fantasy that can never be reached, but test them for yourself, and see the kind of effect they have in the lives of people around you. You just may start a chain reaction.

*Source: Scott, n.d.*

**Figure 6.1: Rachel Scott's essay, "My Ethics, My Codes of Life."**

This essay on personal ethics was written by Rachel Joy Scott. It is impressive on at least three counts. First, it is clearly heartfelt and honest. Rachel obviously believes deeply in what she is reporting. The assignment gave her a platform to acknowledge and articulate ideals at the highest level of her self-system. Second, Rachel's ultimate rule for living is grounded in altruism: "I have this theory that if one person can go out of their way to show compassion, then it will start a chain reaction of the same." Third, her ideals are at a broad enough level to influence almost everything she does. Indeed, her theory would apply to any and every interaction she has with another person.

While the essay in figure 6.1 is impressive in its own right, it is even more so in the context of Rachel's life. Rachel was the first student killed in the tragic school shooting at Columbine High School on April 20, 1999. During her life, she reached out to people in need of compassion and love, performing simple acts of kindness and encouragement for those with social, mental, or physical handicaps. Rachel had a strong premonition—which she shared with her friends and family shortly before her death—that her life would be brief but would impact millions of people. After she died, her father, Darrell Scott, was propelled into the national spotlight as a result of the media and political attention focused on the events at Columbine. Rather than being focused on anger or frustration about what had happened to his daughter, Darrell shared Rachel's ideas about compassion, kindness, forgiveness, and inspiration with large groups of people, eventually founding an organization called Rachel's Challenge. As of 2014, Rachel's story and her ideals have been shared with twenty million people, and some three million students, teachers, and parents are added to that number each year.

While not every student who articulates his or her personal ideals will have the impact on society that Rachel has had, all students will probably benefit from the deep self-analysis. Articulating and confronting our highest-level ideals is probably one of the more powerful human endeavors, as it creates concrete standards of behavior that are difficult to ignore once they have been disclosed.

## Implications for Teaching

While the main focus of this book has been helping teachers understand their inner worlds and how their self-systems affect their decisions and actions in their classrooms, this chapter has highlighted how teachers can teach with their students' inner worlds and self-systems in mind. Teachers can begin by making sure that their students' needs for physiological comfort, safety, belonging, and esteem are met. To help meet students' needs for self-actualization and connection to something greater than the self, teachers can introduce students to concepts such as possible selves, the growth mindset, productive dispositions, and personal ideals. Strategies such as personal projects or capstone projects can bring these constructs together and increase students' awareness of their goals and important beliefs and ideals.

# *Epilogue*

This book is intended to open up a new domain of teacher development—the inner world of our emotions, interpretations, and actions. This trifecta explains virtually everything we do and don't do. Effective teaching is not a simple matter of executing specific behaviors and strategies, because effective teaching is grounded in human relationships. If teachers do not have sound, supportive relationships with their students, the effects of their instructional practices are muted.

At their core, relationships involve emotions, interpretations, and actions. When we are not aware of and in control of these, we operate in a reactionary and mechanistic way and are at the mercy of our unexamined theory of the world. When we are aware of and in control of our emotions, interpretations, and actions, we are capable of transforming any situation we confront into something that we and others experience positively.

When teachers manage their inner worlds, it allows them to have positive interactions with every student. This should be a foundational goal of every teacher, every time they enter the classroom.

# References and Resources

Academy of Achievement. (2010, June 17). *Quincy Jones*. Accessed at www.achievement.org/autodoc/page/jon0bio-1 on January 12, 2015.

Adams, J. S. (1963). Toward an understanding of inequity. *Journal of Abnormal and Social Psychology, 67*(5), 422–436.

Adams, J. S. (1965). Inequity in social exchange. In L. Berkowitz (Ed.), *Advances in experimental social psychology* (Vol. 2, pp. 267–299). New York: Academic Press.

Alderfer, C. P. (1969). An empirical test of a new theory of human needs. *Organizational Behavior and Human Performance, 4*(2), 142–175.

Allport, G. W. (1954). *The nature of prejudice*. Cambridge, MA: Addison-Wesley.

American Psychiatric Association. (2013). *Diagnostic and statistical manual of mental disorders* (5th ed.). Washington, DC: Author.

Anderson, J. R. (1983). *The architecture of cognition*. Cambridge, MA: Harvard University Press.

Anderson, J. R. (1990a). *The adaptive character of thought*. Hillsdale, NJ: Erlbaum.

Anderson, J. R. (1990b). *Cognitive psychology and its implications* (3rd ed.). New York: Freeman.

Anderson, J. R. (Ed.). (1993). *Rules of the mind*. Mahwah, NJ: Erlbaum.

Anderson, J. R. (1995). *Learning and memory: An integrated approach*. New York: Wiley.

Armstrong, T. (2006). *The best schools: How human development research should inform educational practice.* Alexandria, VA: Association for Supervision and Curriculum Development.

Associated Press. (2013, September 20). Dairy Queen employee receives international attention after act of altruism goes viral. *National Post.* Accessed at http://news.nationalpost.com /2013/09/20/dairy-queen-employee-receives-international -attention-after-act-of-altruism-goes-viral/ on October 7, 2014.

ASTROLab. (2006). *Jaymie Mark Matthews (1958– ).* Accessed at astro-canada.ca/_en/a2220.php on January 12, 2015.

Baars, B. J. (2010). Spontaneous repetitive thoughts can be adaptive: Postscript on "mind wandering." *Psychological Bulletin, 136*(2), 208–210.

Baird, B., Smallwood, J., Mrazek, M. D., Kam, J. W. Y., Franklin, M. S., & Schooler, J. W. (2012). Inspired by distraction: Mind wandering facilitates creative incubation. *Psychological Science, 23*(10), 1117–1122.

Barrett, M. (2007). *Children's knowledge, beliefs and feelings about nations and national groups.* New York: Psychology Press.

Benard, B. (2004). *Resiliency: What we have learned.* San Francisco: WestEd.

Berkovich, I., & Eyal, O. (2014). Educational leaders and emotions: An international review of empirical evidence 1992–2012. *Review of Educational Research, 85*(1), 129–167.

Berman, M. G., Nee, D. E., Casement, M., Kim, H. S., Deldin, P., Kross, E., et al. (2011). Neural and behavioral effects of interference resolution in depression and rumination. *Cognitive, Affective, and Behavioral Neuroscience, 11*(1), 85–96.

Bonanno, G. A., & Singer, J. L. (1993). Controlling one's stream of thought through perceptual and reflective processing. In D. M. Wegner & J. W. Pennebaker (Eds.), *Handbook of mental control* (pp. 149–170). Upper Saddle River, NJ: Prentice Hall.

Boy's random act of kindness spreads through community. (2014, August 11). *WWMT*. Accessed at www.wwmt.com/news/features /top-stories/stories/Boy-39-s-random-act-of-kindness-spreads -through-community-12687.shtml#.VDQChmddV8F on October 7, 2014.

Buckley, C. (2007, January 3). Man is rescued by stranger on subway tracks. *The New York Times*. Accessed at www.nytimes.com/2007 /01/03/nyregion/03life.html?_r=0 on January 12, 2015.

Cannon, W. B. (1927). *Bodily changes in pain, hunger, fear and rage*. New York: D. Appleton.

Chalmers, D. J. (1996). *The conscious mind: In search of a fundamental theory*. New York: Oxford University Press.

Chapman, C., & Vagle, N. (2011). *Motivating students: 25 strategies to light the fire of engagement*. Bloomington, IN: Solution Tree Press.

Cohen, J. (1988). *Statistical power analysis for the behavioral sciences* (2nd ed.). Hillsdale, NJ: Erlbaum.

Compton, R. J., Fisher, L. R., Koenig, L. M., McKeown, R., & Muñoz, K. (2003). Relationship between coping styles and perceptual asymmetry. *Journal of Personality and Social Psychology, 84*(5), 1069–1078.

Compton, R. J., & Mintzer, D. A. (2001). Effects of worry and evaluation stress on interhemispheric interaction. *Neuropsychology, 15*(4), 427–433.

Costa, A. L., & Kallick, B. (2014). *Dispositions: Reframing teaching and learning*. Thousand Oaks, CA: Corwin Press.

Coutu, D. L. (2002). How resilience works. *Harvard Business Review, 80*(5), 46–55.

Csikszentmihalyi, M. (1990). *Flow: The psychology of optimal experience*. New York: Harper & Row.

Danielson, C. (2007). *Enhancing professional practice: A framework for teaching* (2nd ed.). Alexandria, VA: Association for Supervision and Curriculum Development.

Davis, R. N., & Nolen-Hoeksema, S. (2000). Cognitive inflexibility among ruminators and nonruminators. *Cognitive Therapy and Research, 24*(6), 699–711.

Deci, E. L. (1995). *Why we do what we do: The dynamics of personal autonomy.* New York: Putnam's Sons.

Deci, E. L., Connell, J. P., & Ryan, R. M. (1989). Self-determination in a work organization. *Journal of Applied Psychology, 74*(4), 580–590.

Deci, E. L., Koestner, R., & Ryan, R. M. (1999). A meta-analytic review of experiments examining the effects of extrinsic rewards on intrinsic motivation. *Psychological Bulletin, 125*(6), 627–668.

Deci, E. L., & Ryan, R. M. (1985). *Intrinsic motivation and self-determination in human behavior.* New York: Plenum.

Deci, E. L., & Ryan, R. M. (1987). The support of autonomy and the control of behavior. *Journal of Personality and Social Psychology, 53*(6), 1024–1037.

Deci, E. L., & Ryan, R. M. (2008a). A self-determination theory approach to psychotherapy: The motivational basis for effective change. *Canadian Psychology, 49*(3), 186–193.

Deci, E. L., & Ryan, R. M. (2008b). Self-determination theory: A macrotheory of human motivation, development, and health. *Canadian Psychology, 49*(3), 182–185.

Degner, J., & Dalege, J. (2013). The apple does not fall far from the tree, or does it? A meta-analysis of parent-child similarity in intergroup attitudes. *Psychological Bulletin, 139*(6), 1270–1304.

Dennett, D. C. (1991). *Consciousness explained.* Boston: Little, Brown.

Descartes, R. (1911). Discourse on the method of rightly conducting the reason and seeking truth in the sciences. In E. S. Haldane & G. R. T. Ross (Eds. and Trans.), *The philosophical works of Descartes* (Vol. 1, pp. 79–130). New York: Cambridge University Press. (Original work published 1637)

Dweck, C. S. (2000). *Self-theories: Their role in motivation, personality, and development.* Philadelphia: Psychology Press.

Einstein, A. (1970). Reply to criticisms. In P. A. Schilpp (Ed.), *Albert Einstein: Philosopher scientist* (pp. 665–688). Evanston, IL: Library of Living Philosophers. (Original work published 1949)

Farley, J. U., Lehmann, D. R., & Ryan, M. J. (1981). Generalizing from "imperfect" replication. *Journal of Business, 54*(4), 597–610.

Finucane, A. M. (2011). The effect of fear and anger on selective attention. *Emotion, 11*(4), 970–974.

Frankl, V. E. (1958, September 13). The search for meaning. *Saturday Review.* Accessed at www.unz.org/Pub/SaturdayRev -1958sep13?View=PDF on January 8, 2015.

Frankl, V. E. (1963). *Man's search for meaning: An introduction to logotherapy.* New York: Simon & Schuster.

Fredrickson, B. L. (1998). What good are positive emotions? *Review of General Psychology, 2*(3), 300–319.

Fredrickson, B. L. (2001). The role of positive emotions in positive psychology: The broaden-and-build theory of positive emotions. *American Psychologist, 56*(3), 218–226.

Gable, P. A., & Harmon-Jones, E. (2011). Attentional consequences of pregoal and postgoal positive affects. *Emotion, 11*(6), 1358–1367.

Gamble, L. (2014). One man's heartwarming random acts of kindness. *Stuff.* Accessed at www.stuff.co.nz/life-style/beauty /beauty-news/10420363/One-mans-heartwarming-random-acts -of-kindness on October 7, 2014.

Garmezy, N. (1974). Children at risk: The search for the antecedents of schizophrenia—Part II: Ongoing research programs, issues, and intervention. *Schizophrenia Bulletin, 1*(9), 55–125.

Glasser, W. (1965). *Reality therapy.* New York: Harper & Row.

Glasser, W. (1969). *Schools without failure.* New York: Harper & Row.

Glasser, W. (1981). *Stations of the mind: New directions for reality therapy.* New York: Harper & Row.

Glossary of Education Reform. (2014, February). *Capstone project.* Accessed at http://edglossary.org/capstone-project/ on October 7, 2014.

Gould, C. E., & Edelstein, B. A. (2010). Worry, emotion control, and anxiety control in older and younger adults. *Journal of Anxiety Disorders, 24*(7), 759–766.

Hargreaves, A. (1998). The emotional politics of teaching and teacher development: With implications for educational leadership. *International Journal of Leadership in Education, 1*(4), 315–336.

Harter, S. (1999). *The construction of the self: A developmental perspective.* New York: Guilford Press.

Hattie, J. (2012). *Visible learning for teachers: Maximizing impact on learning.* New York: Routledge.

Heidegger, M. (1977). Letter on humanism. In D. F. Krell (Ed.), *Basic writings* (pp. 213–265). London: Routledge.

Hertel, P. T. (1998). Relation between rumination and impaired memory in dysphoric moods. *Journal of Abnormal Psychology, 107*(1), 166–172.

Herzberg, F., Mausner, B., & Snyderman, B. B. (1967). *The motivation to work* (2nd ed.). New York: Wiley.

Holland, J. H., Holyoak, K. J., Nisbett, R. E., & Thagard, P. R. (1986). *Induction: Processes of inference, learning, and discovery.* Cambridge, MA: MIT Press.

James Cameron Online. (n.d.). *Biography.* Accessed at www.james camerononline.com/Biography.htm on January 12, 2015.

Jensen, E. (2005). *Teaching with the brain in mind* (2nd ed., rev. ed.). Alexandria, VA: Association for Supervision and Curriculum Development.

Joormann, J. (2006). Differential effects of rumination and dysphoria on the inhibition of irrelevant emotional material: Evidence from a negative priming task. *Cognitive Therapy and Research, 30,* 149–160.

Joormann, J., & Gotlib, I. H. (2008). Updating the contents of working memory in depression: Interference from irrelevant negative material. *Journal of Abnormal Psychology, 117*(1), 182–192.

Joormann, J., Levens, S. M., & Gotlib, I. H. (2011). Sticky thoughts: Depression and rumination are associated with difficulties manipulating emotional material in working memory. *Psychological Science, 22*(8), 979–983.

Joormann, J., & Tran, T. B. (2009). Rumination and intentional forgetting of emotional material. *Cognition and Emotion, 23*(6), 1233–1246.

Kelly, E. F., Kelly, E. W., Crabtree, A., Gauld, A., Grosso, M., & Greyson, B. (2007). *Irreducible mind: Toward a psychology for the 21st century.* Lanham, MD: Rowman & Littlefield.

Kena, G., Aud, S., Johnson, F., Wang, X., Zhang, J., Rathbun, A., et al. (2014). *The condition of education 2014.* Accessed at http://nces.ed.gov/pubs2014/2014083.pdf on September 5, 2014.

Kersey, C. (1998). *Unstoppable: 45 powerful stories of perseverance and triumph from people just like you.* Naperville, IL: Sourcebooks.

Kessler, R. (2000). *The soul of education: Helping students find connection, compassion, and character at school.* Alexandria, VA: Association for Supervision and Curriculum Development.

Kidder, R. M. (2005). *Moral courage.* New York: Morrow.

Killingsworth, M. A., & Gilbert, D. T. (2010). A wandering mind is an unhappy mind. *Science, 330,* 932.

Kim, M., & Hunter, J. E. (1993a). Attitude-behavior relations: A meta-analysis of attitudinal relevance and topic. *Journal of Communication, 43*(1), 101–142.

Kim, M., & Hunter, J. E. (1993b). Relationships among attitudes, behavioral intentions, and behavior: A meta-analysis of past research, part 2. *Communication Research, 20*(3), 331–364.

Knight, J. (2013). *High-impact instruction: A framework for great teaching.* Thousand Oaks, CA: Corwin Press.

Kolmogorov, A. N. (n.d.). Quote. In American Society for Cybernetics (Ed.), *Defining 'cybernetics.'* Accessed at www.asc -cybernetics.org/foundations/definitions.htm on November 11, 2014.

Kraus, S. J. (1995). Attitudes and the prediction of behavior: A meta-analysis of the empirical literature. *Personality and Social Psychology Bulletin, 21*(1), 58–75.

LeDoux, J. E. (2002). *Synaptic self: How our brains become who we are.* New York: Viking.

Lee, G. (2006). *Courage: The backbone of leadership.* San Francisco: Jossey-Bass.

Levy, S. (2013). Google's Larry Page on why moon shots matter. *Wired.* Accessed at www.wired.com/2013/01/ff-qa-larry-page/all on October 7, 2014.

Linnenbrink, E. A. (2007). The role of affect in student learning: A multi-dimensional approach to considering the interaction of affect, motivation, and engagement. In P. A. Schutz & R. Pekrun (Eds.), *Emotion in education* (pp. 107–124). Burlington, MA: Academic Press.

Liston, D., & Garrison, J. (2004). Introduction: Love revived and examined. In D. Liston & J. Garrison (Eds.), *Teaching, learning, and loving: Reclaiming passion in educational practice* (pp. 1–19). New York: RoutledgeFalmer.

Lord, C. G., & Taylor, C. A. (2009). Biased assimilation: Effects of assumptions and expectations on the interpretation of new evidence. *Social and Personality Psychology Compass, 3*(5), 827–841.

Macrorie, K. (1988). *The I-Search paper.* Portsmouth, NH: Boynton/ Cook.

Markman, H. J., Stanley, S. M., & Blumberg, S. L. (2010). *Fighting for your marriage: A deluxe revised edition of the classic best seller for enhancing marriage and preventing divorce* (3rd ed.). San Francisco: Jossey-Bass.

Markus, H., & Nurius, P. (1986). Possible selves. *American Psychologist, 41*(9), 954–969.

Marzano, R. J. (with Marzano, J. S., & Pickering, D. J.). (2003a). *Classroom management that works: Research-based strategies for every teacher.* Alexandria, VA: Association for Supervision and Curriculum Development.

Marzano, R. J. (2003b). *What works in schools: Translating research into action.* Alexandria, VA: Association for Supervision and Curriculum Development.

Marzano, R. J. (2007). *The art and science of teaching: A comprehensive framework for effective instruction.* Alexandria, VA: Association for Supervision and Curriculum Development.

Marzano, R. J. (2013). Defusing out-of-control behavior. *Educational Leadership, 71*(4), 82–83.

Marzano, R. J., Brandt, R. S., Hughes, C. S., Jones, B. F., Presseisen, B. Z., Rankin, S. C., et al. (1988). *Dimensions of thinking: A framework for curriculum and instruction.* Alexandria, VA: Association for Supervision and Curriculum Development.

Marzano, R. J., Gaddy, B. B., Foseid, M. C., Foseid, M. P., & Marzano, J. S. (2005). *A handbook for classroom management that works.* Alexandria, VA: Association for Supervision and Curriculum Development.

Marzano, R. J., & Heflebower, T. (2012). *Teaching & assessing 21st century skills.* Bloomington, IN: Marzano Research.

Marzano, R. J., & Marzano, J. S. (1987). *Contextual thinking: The most basic of the cognitive skills* (Tech. Rep.). Aurora, CO: Mid-continent Regional Educational Laboratory. (ERIC Document Reproduction Service No. ED286634)

Marzano, R. J., & Marzano, J. S. (1989). Toward a cognitive theory of commitment and its implications for therapy. *Psychotherapy in Private Practice, 6*(4), 69–81.

Marzano, R. J., & Marzano, J. S. (2003). The key to classroom management. *Educational Leadership, 61*(1), 6–13.

Marzano, R. J., & Marzano, J. S. (2010). The inner game of teaching. In R. J. Marzano (Ed.), *On excellence in teaching* (pp. 345–367). Bloomington, IN: Solution Tree Press.

Marzano, R. J., & Pickering, D. J. (with Heflebower, T.). (2011). *The highly engaged classroom*. Bloomington, IN: Marzano Research.

Marzano, R. J., Pickering, D. J., & Pollock, J. E. (2001). *Classroom instruction that works: Research-based strategies for increasing student achievement*. Alexandria, VA: Association for Supervision and Curriculum Development.

Maslow, A. H. (1943). A theory of human motivation. *Psychological Review, 50*, 370–396.

Maslow, A. H. (1954). *Motivation and personality*. New York: Harper.

Mathews, A. (1990). Why worry? The cognitive structure of anxiety. *Behavior Research and Therapy, 28*(6), 455–468.

McCain, J. (2004). *Why courage matters: The way to a braver life*. New York: Random House.

McCaul, K. D., & Mullens, A. B. (2003). Affect, thought and self-protective health behavior: The case of worry and cancer screening. In J. Suls & K. A. Wallston (Eds.), *Social psychological foundations of health and illness* (pp. 137–168). Malden, MA: Blackwell.

McClelland, D. C. (1965). Toward a theory of motive acquisition. *American Psychologist, 20*(5), 321–333.

McCombs, B. L., & Marzano, R. J. (1990). Putting the self in self-regulated learning: The self as agent in integrating will and skill. *Educational Psychologist, 25*(1), 51–69.

McKay, M., Davis, M., & Fanning, P. (2011). *Thoughts & feelings: Taking control of your moods & your life* (4th ed.). Oakland, CA: New Harbinger.

Mrazek, M. D., Smallwood, J., & Schooler, J. W. (2012). Mindfulness and mind-wandering: Finding convergence through opposing constructs. *Emotion, 12*(3), 442–448.

Nemours Foundation/KidsHealth, Department of Health Education and Recreation, & National Association of Health Education Centers. (2007). *KidsHealth KidsPoll—What do kids worry about? (2007) Summary of findings.* Accessed at http://kidshealth.org /media/kidspoll/related/worry_summary_of_findings_(07)_CE.pdf on October 6, 2014.

Novick, B., Kress, J. S., & Elias, M. J. (2002). *Building learning communities with character: How to integrate academic, social, and emotional learning.* Alexandria, VA: Association for Supervision and Curriculum Development.

Orlick, T. (2008). *In pursuit of excellence: How to win in sport and life through mental training* (4th ed.). Champaign, IL: Human Kinetics.

O'Shaughnessy, J. (2009). *Interpretation in social life, social science, and marketing.* New York: Routledge.

Oyserman, D., Terry, K., & Bybee, D. (2002). A possible selves intervention to enhance school involvement. *Journal of Adolescence, 25,* 313–326.

Paivio, A. (1969). Mental imagery in associative learning and memory. *Psychological Review, 76*(3), 241–263.

Paivio, A. (1971). *Imagery and verbal processes.* New York: Holt, Rinehart & Winston.

Peale, N. V. (1952). *The power of positive thinking.* New York: Prentice Hall.

Phan, T. (2003). Life in school: Narratives of resiliency among Vietnamese-Canadian youths. *Adolescence, 38*(151), 555–566.

Piaget, J. (1964). Relations between affectivity and intelligence in the mental development of the child. In *Sorbonne courses.* Paris: University Documentation Center.

Popham, W. J. (2009). *Instruction that measures up: Successful teaching in the age of accountability.* Alexandria, VA: Association for Supervision and Curriculum Development.

Purdy, A. (2011). Living beyond limits [Video file]. *TEDxOrangeCoast*. Accessed at www.ted.com/talks/amy_purdy_living_beyond_limits#t-226666 on October 7, 2014.

Randall, D. M., & Wolff, J. A. (1994). The time interval in the intention-behavior relationship: Meta-analysis. *British Journal of Social Psychology, 33*(4), 405–418.

Reece, K. (2014). Baytown firefighters' random act of kindness goes viral. *KVUE*. Accessed at www.kvue.com/story/news/state/2014/09/02/baytown-firefighters-random-act-of-kindness-goes-viral/14961097/ on October 7, 2014.

Remedy Health Media. (2015). The toll of untreated depression. *Health After 50*. Accessed at www.healthafter50.com/alerts/depression_anxiety/Consequences-of-Untreated-Depression_6908-1.html on January 8, 2015.

Richard, F. D., Bond, C. F., Jr., & Stokes-Zoota, J. J. (2003). One hundred years of social psychology quantitatively described. *Review of General Psychology, 7*(4), 331–363.

Richardson, P. W., Karabenick, S. A., & Watt, H. M. G. (Eds.). (2014). *Teacher motivation: Theory and practice*. New York: Routledge.

Robers, S., Kemp, J., & Truman, J. (2013). *Indicators of school crime and safety: 2012*. Accessed at http://nces.ed.gov/pubs2013/2013036.pdf on September 5, 2014.

Roemer, L., & Borkovec, T. D. (1993). Worry: Unwanted cognitive activity that controls unwanted somatic experience. In D. M. Wegner & J. W. Pennebaker (Eds.), *Handbook of mental control* (pp. 220–238). Upper Saddle River, NJ: Prentice Hall.

Roeser, R. W., Schonert-Reichl, K. A., Jha, A., Cullen, M., Wallace, L., Wilensky, R., et al. (2013). Mindfulness training and reductions in teacher stress and burnout: Results from two randomized, waitlist-control field trials. *Journal of Educational Psychology, 105*(3), 787–804.

Rubin, L. B. (1996). *The transcendent child: Tales of triumph over the past*. New York: Basic Books.

Ryan, R. M., & Deci, E. L. (2000). Self-determination theory and the facilitation of intrinsic motivation, social development, and well-being. *American Psychologist, 55*(1), 68–78.

Saphier, J., Haley-Speca, M. A., & Gower, R. (2008). *The skillful teacher: Building your teaching skills* (6th ed.). Acton, MA: Research for Better Teaching.

Schank, R. C., & Abelson, R. (1977). *Scripts, plans, goals, and understanding: An inquiry into human knowledge structures.* Hillsdale, NJ: Erlbaum.

Schreck, M. K. (2011). *You've got to reach them to teach them: Hard facts about the soft skills of student engagement.* Bloomington, IN: Solution Tree Press.

Schutz, P. A., & Pekrun, R. (Eds.). (2007). *Emotion in education.* Burlington, MA: Academic Press.

Scott, D., & Marzano, R. J. (2014). *Awaken the learner: Finding the source of effective education.* Bloomington, IN: Marzano Research.

Scott, R. (n.d.). *My ethics, my codes of life.* Accessed at www .rachelschallenge.org/essay on March 5, 2015.

Seligman, M. E. P. (2006). *Learned optimism: How to change your mind and your life.* New York: Vintage Books.

Shapiro, F. (1996). Eye movement desensitization and reprocessing (EMDR): Evaluation of controlled PTSD research. *Journal of Behavior Therapy and Experimental Psychiatry, 27*(3), 209–218.

Sheppard, B. H., Hartwick, J., & Warshaw, P. R. (1988). The theory of reasoned action: A meta-analysis of past research with recommendations for modifications and future research. *Journal of Consumer Research, 15*(3), 325–343.

Silver, H. F., Strong, R. W., & Perini, M. J. (2007). *The strategic teacher: Selecting the right research-based strategy for every lesson.* Alexandria, VA: Association for Supervision and Curriculum Development.

Skinner, B. F. (1938). *The behavior of organisms: An experimental analysis.* New York: Appleton-Century.

Skinner, B. F. (1953). *Science and human behavior.* New York: Macmillan.

Skinner, E. A., Kindermann, T. A., Connell, J. P., & Wellborn, J. G. (2009). Engagement and disaffection as organizational constructs in the dynamics of motivational development. In K. R. Wentzel & A. Wigfield (Eds.), *Handbook of motivation at school* (pp. 223–245). New York: Routledge.

Smallwood, J. (2013). Distinguishing how from why the mind wanders: A process-occurrence framework for self-generated mental activity. *Psychological Bulletin, 139*(3), 519–535.

Smallwood, J., & Schooler, J. W. (2013). The restless mind. *Psychology of Consciousness: Theory, Research, and Practice, 1*(S), 130–149.

Smith, F. (2004). *Understanding reading: A psycholinguistic analysis of reading and learning to read* (6th ed.). Mahwah, NJ: Erlbaum. (Original work published 1971)

Smith, L. (2009, November 22). Warren Buffett's frugal, so why aren't you? *Investopedia.* Accessed at www.investopedia.com /articles/financialcareers/10/buffett-frugal.asp on January 12, 2015.

Southwick, S. M., & Charney, D. S. (2012). *Resilience: The science of mastering life's greatest challenges.* New York: Cambridge University Press.

Tavris, C. (1989). *Anger: The misunderstood emotion* (Rev. ed.). New York: Touchstone.

Thrash, T. M., & Elliot, A. J. (2003). Inspiration as a psychological construct. *Journal of Personality and Social Psychology, 84*(4), 871–889.

Thrash, T. M., & Elliot, A. J. (2004). Inspiration: Core characteristics, component processes, antecedents, and function. *Journal of Personality and Social Psychology, 87*(6), 957–973.

Thrash, T. M., Elliot, A. J., Maruskin, L. A., & Cassidy, S. E. (2010). Inspiration and the promotion of well-being: Tests of causality and mediation. *Journal of Personality and Social Psychology, 98*(3), 488–506.

Tom Monaghan in 30 minutes or less. (2008). *Entrepreneur.* Accessed at www.entrepreneur.com/article/197674 on October 7, 2014.

Turk, D. C., & Winter, F. (2006). *The pain survival guide: How to reclaim your life.* Washington, DC: American Psychological Association.

van Dijk, T. A. (1980). *Macrostructures: An interdisciplinary study of global structures in discourse, interaction, and cognition.* Hillsdale, NJ: Erlbaum.

Vroom, V. H. (1964). *Work and motivation.* New York: Wiley.

Vygotsky, L. S. (1962). *Thought and language.* Cambridge, MA: MIT Press.

Watkins, E., & Brown, R. G. (2002). Rumination and executive function in depression: An experimental study. *Journal of Neurology, Neurosurgery and Psychiatry, 72,* 400–402.

Watkins, E. R., & Nolen-Hoeksema, S. (2014). A habit-goal framework of depressive rumination. *Journal of Abnormal Psychology, 123*(1), 24–34.

Wegner, D. M., & Erber, R. (1993). Social foundations of mental control. In D. M. Wegner & J. W. Pennebaker (Eds.), *Handbook of mental control* (pp. 36–56). Upper Saddle River, NJ: Prentice Hall.

Wegner, D. M., & Pennebaker, J. W. (1993). Changing our minds: An introduction to mental control. In D. M. Wegner & J. W. Pennebaker (Eds.), *Handbook of mental control* (pp. 1–12). Upper Saddle River, NJ: Prentice Hall.

Wessler, S. L. (2003). *The respectful school: How educators and students can conquer hate and harassment.* Alexandria, VA: Association for Supervision and Curriculum Development.

Whitmer, A. J., & Banich, M. T. (2011). Repetitive thought and reversal learning deficits. *Cognitive Therapy and Research, 36*(6), 714–721.

Whitmer, A. J., Frank, M. J., & Gotlib, I. H. (2012). Sensitivity to reward and punishment in major depressive disorder: Effects of rumination and of single versus multiple experiences. *Cognition and Emotion, 26*(8), 1475–1485.

Whitmer, A. J., & Gotlib, I. H. (2013). An attentional scope model of rumination. *Psychological Bulletin, 139*(5), 1036–1061.

Wiener, N. (1961). *Cybernetics: Or control and communication in the animal and the machine* (2nd ed.). Cambridge, MA: MIT Press.

Wiggins, G., & McTighe, J. (2005). *Understanding by design* (2nd ed.). Alexandria, VA: Association for Supervision and Curriculum Development.

Williams, K. C. (2012). *Creating physical and emotional security in schools* (2nd ed.). Bloomington, IN: Solution Tree Press.

Wood, W., Quinn, J. M., & Kashy, D. A. (2002). Habits in everyday life: Thought, emotion, and action. *Journal of Personality and Social Psychology, 83*(6), 1281–1297.

Zimmerman, R. S., & Vernberg, D. (1994). Models of preventive health behavior: Comparison, critique, and meta-analysis. *Advances in Medical Sociology, 4*, 45–67.

Zivot, M. T., Cohen, A. L., & Kapucu, A. (2013). Modeling the effect of mood on dimensional attention during categorization. *Emotion, 13*(4), 703–710.

Zmuda, A., Kuklis, R., & Kline, E. (2004). *Transforming schools: Creating a culture of continuous improvement*. Alexandria, VA: Association for Supervision and Curriculum Development.

# *Index*

## A

Abelson, R., 25–26

actions, intentions versus, 4–5

Allport, G. W., 22

altruism, 90–93

analysis phase, 10, 11, 40, 84, 85

Anderson, J. R., 48, 65

anger, 18–21

*Anger: The Misunderstood Emotion* (Tavris), 18

approach motivation, 73

attitudes

    relationship between behavior and, 3–4

    relationship between parents' and children's, 22–23

autonomy (freedom), sense of, 87–88

Autrey, W., 91

awareness phase, 10, 40, 84, 85

## B

Baars, B. J., 53

Barrett, M., 23

Baytown fire fighters, 92

behavior

    *See also* teacher behaviors

    mechanistic, 8–9

reactionary, 9

relationship between attitudes and, 3–4

belonging within a community, 29, 74, 98–100

Benard, B., 66

Berkovich, I., 3

blaming, 57

Blumberg, S. L., 27

Bonanno, G. A., 54

Bond, C. F., Jr., 3, 4

Borkovec, T. D., 61–62

Buffett, W., 114

Bustos, M., 93

Bybee, D., 102

## C

Cameron, J., 109

Cannon, W. B., 17

capstone project, 116

Cassidy, S. E., 73

catastrophizing, 57

categories, formation of, 22–23

Charney, D. S., 16, 17, 18, 66–67, 71–72, 89–91

choice phase, 10, 11, 40, 84–85, 86

comfort, 29, 74, 95–98

# Tap into the inner world of students

Create a compassionate, caring school environment. Examine how a change in teaching philosophy can help awaken the passion for learning in students. Learn how to promote kindness in the classroom, and understand the power of stories in engaging students. Explore research-based strategies to enhance teacher-student and peer relationships. Discover how to inspire purpose, reach students' hearts, and cultivate student security, identity, and belonging.

# Order today!
marzanoresearch.com  |  888.849.0851

MARZANO Research

# Transform teaching
## using inner thoughts and feelings

 Signature PD Service

## Managing the Inner World of Teaching Workshop

Expand your ability to maintain a positive mindset in the classroom by cultivating a deeper awareness of your emotions, interpretations, and responses as a teacher. In this workshop, Robert J. Marzano and Jana S. Marzano combine their backgrounds in educational research and psychotherapy to present a comprehensive model of how the human mind operates. The heart of that model involves three dynamic processes: (1) our emotional responses, (2) our interpretations, and (3) our actions. Each of those processes affects the moment-by-moment decisions that teachers make in the classroom.

### Learning Outcomes

- Gain an awareness of emotional responses and how they affect interpretations and reactions.
- Discover a three-phase management process designed to promote awareness, analysis, and choice.
- Engage in retrospective and real-time practice exercises for managing the inner world.
- Explore mental strategies that encourage mindfulness and patterns of positive thinking.
- Discover how to cultivate students' understanding of their personal values, goals, and the power of a positive mindset.

# Learn more!
**marzanoresearch.com/OnsitePD  |  888.849.0851**